Making Money With God

Learning To Hear The Holy Spirit

A. Bruce Wells

authorHOUSE®

AuthorHouse™
1663 Liberty Drive
Bloomington, IN 47403
www.authorhouse.com
Phone: 1-800-839-8640

© 2011 A. Bruce Wells. All rights reserved.

No part of this book may be reproduced, stored in a retrieval system, or transmitted by any means without the written permission of the author.

First published by AuthorHouse   5/26/2011

ISBN: 978-1-4567-5744-1 (sc)
ISBN: 978-1-4567-5743-4 (hc)
ISBN: 978-1-4567-5742-7 (e)

Library of Congress Control Number: 2011907077

Printed in the United States of America

*Any people depicted in stock imagery provided by Thinkstock are models, and such images are being used for illustrative purposes only.
Certain stock imagery © Thinkstock.*

This book is printed on acid-free paper.

Because of the dynamic nature of the Internet, any web addresses or links contained in this book may have changed since publication and may no longer be valid. The views expressed in this work are solely those of the author and do not necessarily reflect the views of the publisher, and the publisher hereby disclaims any responsibility for them.

"Money Answers All Things…"

Solomon, Eccl. 10:19

"Whoever said, 'Money can't buy happiness,' never watched *The Price Is Right*."

Bruce Wells

ATTENTION!

DO YOU KNOW THAT THE FOLLOWING IS AN **ABSOLUTE TRUTH: THE HOLY SPIRIT KNOWS EVERYTHING** ABOUT EVERY PERSON, BUSINESS, STOCK, HOUSE, BOND, INVESTMENT, COMMODITY, POLITICIAN, CAR, CHURCH, JOB, SITUATION, PROBLEM, POTENTIAL DANGER, AND/OR ANYTHING THING ELSE ON THIS PLANET THAT COULD POSSIBLY BE OF INTEREST TO YOU?

DO YOU ALSO KNOW THAT THE HOLY SPIRIT IS WILLING TO SHARE INFORMATION WITH YOU IF YOU'RE WILLING TO LEARN HOW TO HEAR HIM? AND DO YOU KNOW THAT HE IS WILLING TO LIVE EVERY MINUTE OF EVERYDAY WITH YOU, AND THAT HE NEVER MAKES MISTAKES?

IF YOU ARE UNAWARE OF THE REALITY OF THESE FACTS, BY THE TIME YOU FINISH THIS BOOK, A NEW REFRESHING RELATIONSHIP WITH THE HOLY SPIRIT (ALMIGHTY GOD) MIGHT BECOME THE MAJOR DRIVING FORCE IN YOUR LIFE. IF YOU DON'T WANT THIS, STOP READING NOW.

THE PUBLISHERS OF THIS BOOK, OR ANY OF THEIR ASSOCIATES, CAN NOT BE HELD RESPONSIBLE, OR LIABLE, FOR ANY OF THE POSITIVE CHANGES THAT MAY OCCUR IN YOUR LIFE DUE TO THE INFORMATION CONTAINED IN THIS BOOK. PLEASE READ WITH CAUTION; THIS BOOK HAS BEEN KNOWN TO HAVE TREMENDOUS OPTIMISTIC INFLUENCE ON THE WAY MOST READERS THINK.

TABLE OF CONTENTS

Preface	xi
Chapter 1 Wet Your Appetite	1
Chapter 2 Qualifications	14
Chapter 3 Who Is This For?	37
Chapter 4 Let's Get Started	45
Chapter 5 Learning to Hear God?	64
Chapter 6 Should Christians Have Wealth?	93
Chapter 7 Verses	123
About the Author	129

PREFACE

NOTHING WILL CHANGE UNLESS YOU CHANGE IT; AND YOU WON'T CHANGE UNTIL YOU CHANGE YOUR THINKING.

So, I'm sitting at a busy intersection on U.S. 1 in a small town in south Florida, waiting for the light to change. As I wait, a cargo truck with the word *Silver* in the name of the company pulls up on my left and suddenly, I sense this strange, visual attraction to the word "silver." I suspect that this "visual fixation" is from the Holy Spirit, but I'm not sure. I've experienced this sort of thing before when God was trying to show me something, but these things can vary in intensity. This time, it was not exactly overwhelming. Then I think, "If God is causing this, what does it mean?

As I ponder this experience for a couple of seconds, a second truck pulls up on my right and low and behold, it has the word *Gold* in its company name. Once again, I experience the same attention drawing phenomenon as I become more aware that this episode is from the Lord. It's difficult to describe such an experience, other than to say it is similar to when you see someone in a crowd who catches your attention, as if you recognize this person, but you just can't seem to recall when and where. But, this experience also had an anointing (a tangible, spiritual presence) attached, and it felt like God was trying to impart something.

Then the meaning of the whole experience hit me like a slap in the face. Normally, two trucks with these words would mean nothing because these are common words that we see everyday. But, when the Holy Spirit is trying to get your attention, things can just seem to jump out at you because God is setting an opportunity before you, and He doesn't want you to miss it. Such attention grabbers are like seeing a *highlighted* word on a page.

Earlier that morning, I had been praying and asking God to show me a good stock to trade (this is not a book about stocks), a prayer I had been praying daily for some time. Make sure you caught that, because these experiences don't just randomly happen. They are the result of real prayer, and real seeking, from real believers. Some would laugh at such a notion, or the experience above, but the Holy Spirit is a real person who knows how to speak to us. Also, He knows everything about every person, every problem, and every situation on the planet. It would greatly behoove you to learn to recognize and listen to His voice. He has your best interest at heart, and will never lead you astray.

The Holy Spirit knows when there is danger ahead, or when someone is lying to you. He knows if that person you're trying to fall in love with is a good person, or the devil in disguise. He knows if the investment you're about to make is a good idea or a disaster. He knows the secrets of every heart you'll ever come in contact with. He knew all along that Bernie Madoff was a swindler. He didn't just find out when the story broke in the news. But, apparently, most of the good people who were Mr. Madoff's clients, didn't know the Holy Spirit, or they would have run the other way. And, the Holy Spirit knows exactly where the money is that you need for you and your family. Are you willing to get to know Him?

Just a couple of days ago, I heard a minister on the radio making fun of Christians who claim to hear, and/or actually be led by, the Holy Spirit. But just because this isn't happening to someone who probably doesn't believe in it anyway, doesn't mean that it's not happening to others. I'm always amazed at ministers who take a stand against something because it hasn't happened to them. Even though they may know little or nothing about the Holy Spirit, they're determined to tell us what's real, and what isn't. These things happen according "faith," not according to "unbelief" (the refusal to believe).

The sharing of inaccurate opinions happens frequently when it comes to the supernatural things of the Spirit. I've never been to Tibet, but I'm not going to go on the radio and claim that it doesn't exist just because I've never been there. You would have to ignore dozens of scriptures to accept any watered down teaching that removes the supernatural from the Christian life. I prefer to listen to men and women who have experience and know God intimately, over those who just lecture according to the restrictive teachings of "their camp." Ministers often have no real experience at all when it comes to the supernatural.

Obviously, many of God's servants in the Bible were strategically led by God, angels, miraculous signs, and prophecy; but this radio preacher has thrown the baby out with the bath water just because some Christians have been reckless with the things of God. Or he's afraid of scaring away some of his sophisticated members. This is a huge mistake because such an attitude blocks the real thing. It's a good thing that Peter and Paul didn't sit under such teaching as new believers. Peter never would have gone to Cornelius' house, and Paul never would have gone to Macedonia. Both men were led by visions, dreams, and other forms of hearing God.

Without the precious Holy Spirit, functionally, we're just another religion, and yes, you should be able to "feel" His presence from time to time. Later, I'll quote some really good promises concerning God's leading to stir your faith, and even some where God promises to show you the future. Do you think knowing the future could help you make money? It sure helped Joseph in Egypt. How many of us have watched time travel movies and dreamed of going back in time to give ourselves some useful information? Well, if you know the Holy Spirit, you actually can gain information about the future because He can see it now. And if you act on that information, you won't have to wish you could go back and do it over.

Even without God's help, billionaire George Soros made his money by predicting currency fluctuations simply based on the way world events were lining up. How much more should we be able to profit *with* God's help? I recently heard a Christian friend say, "God is going to *raise up* a modern day Joseph to help his people." This is so typical of erroneous church thinking in our day. God wants each and everyone one of us to be as wise as Joseph, not just one special person.

The church never seems to get the revelation that every person who has really been "born again," actually has Jesus living inside them. This is a much better situation than Joseph had. If some other Christian rises to great wealth, do you really think he or she is going to help you personally? Let me know how that works out.

xiii

EVERYONE THINKS THEY'RE RIGHT

You know, all churches "think" they're teaching the right things about the Holy Spirit, but are they actually experiencing tangible, Bible types of manifestations in their midst? And I mean the real thing(s), not the flaky stuff that drives thinking people away. God likes to manifest Himself where there is real faith, and "real faith" comes by right teaching. "Faith comes by hearing," when the right things are taught. (Romans 10) Or, faith leaves when the wrong things are taught, which is fairly common. And the hearers of the wrong stuff are left wondering why God never shows up, or why they can't get what they want, or need.

Every answer any Christian is looking for is a matter of faith, understanding, or being able to hear God; but most people are usually led to believe that they just didn't _____ enough. You fill in the blank. But, if you plant the right faith seeds in your mind, eventually you'll have a strong faith tree in the midst your thinking; or you'll have whatever else you've been listening to.

Maybe you heard it in church, but that doesn't mean it's "gospel." I've watched many Christians say "amen" to churchy sounding things that aren't even close to being the gospel. They hear religious sounding clichés again and again and the repetition eventually makes them think they're hearing the truth. But in reality, such thinking often effectively repels the truth. False doctrine and church tradition can work like a vaccination. The injection of the dead virus builds up a resistance to the real thing. It takes work and diligence to think right, especially when you've been trained in religion instead of redemption.

So, what was the "silver & gold" thing all about? Well, that same morning I had been looking over several stocks that had been on my radar screen for several days, and one of them was a Chinese mining stock (symbol CHNR) that produced silver and gold. Again, these are common words in the investing world, but that morning I had that same attention grabbing feeling that I had at the intersection, only I had forgotten about it until the two trucks pulled up. Then the Holy Spirit instantly brought the Chinese stock to my remembrance as I sat at that light. Now it was all falling together. Again, this was all happening because I had been fervently asking God for a leading.

And not only did God do the "two trucks" thing for me, but He again confirmed the stock later that day when I met with a friend of

xiv

mine. As I pulled into the driveway behind my friend's pickup truck, I noticed a large box in the back with the letters C-H-I-N-A, as if they were staring me right in the face, and again I got that same inward witness from the Holy Spirit. We should never act on such things without that true, Holy Spirit, inward witness, because wishful thinking can get us into trouble. We'll say more about that later.

What happened next? Well, to keep the story short, the following day (not years later like many investments take), CHNR made an unbelievable jump from a little over $12 per share, to $20. This alone would have been a one day "homerun trade," but the huge jump attracted other investors and the stock kept increasing at the rate of about $6 per day until it reached $49 per share. Then the buying stopped. How would you like to have known about such a stock move BEFORE it happened?

The same God who told me, can, and will, tell you if you're hungry enough. And always remember this: **There is always something, somewhere, getting ready to move.** Prices, supplies, demand, and many other variables are constantly changing. This movement causes nonstop profit opportunities for those who have learned to watch, and listen.

The incident above is a true story, and in the following pages you're going to learn how money making opportunities are happening everyday all over the world, and how the precious Holy Spirit knows about every one of them, in advance. This is the ultimate, reliable "inside information," and it's totally legal and available to anyone who truly knows God! Christians should be the best money makers in the world, instead of the pitiful, distressed people they often seem to be. It's not a sin to be in a position of suffering, or to be beat up and beat down, but who in their right mind wants to stay that way?

There are millions of Christians who can't pay their bills, buy a decent car, send their kids to college, or do any of the things they dream about. It is also estimated that over 40% of the housing foreclosures in this country (the USA), caused by government interference, are happening to born again Christians. This is something that is totally out of order.

Make no mistake; no matter whose face(s) you want to put on the blame of the present financial meltdown, it was caused by government intervention in our banking system(s), government over spending, and debt. No one can spend more than they take in and stay out of trouble, not even Uncle Sam. That is exactly what has put us, and the rest of the world, in the middle of this crisis. It is really no more complicated than that, although they want us to believe our problems are very complex. Any other reasoning only addresses the symptoms, not the cause.

GOD WANTS TO HELP YOU

Wouldn't it be great if everyone on the planet received an equal, sufficient, daily, allotment; and if anyone squandered theirs, they would only have to wait until the next morning for more? This is kind of the way God did things in the wilderness when He supplied manna everyday. Their clothes didn't wear out, and they had fresh food every morning. Gee, if you're under the pressures of this demanding world, being in the wilderness back then might not sound so bad right now. But, if they were that well cared for back then, and we have a better covenant now, surely God has a plan for each of us to be sufficiently taken care of.

God has provided more than enough for everyone on this planet, but the problem is ignorance, and not everyone knows God personally. Governments may try to control distribution, which is a farce, but God's plan is to listen to, and follow, Him. Otherwise, people will generally make a mess of everything. But, God has not left His people without a plan, or a way to overcome participating in this rat race for money.

If you can get it through your head that God knows how to make money, and that He wants to help you, AND WILL; you can learn to rise above the financially drowning crowd of Christians who are still trying to earn God's approval while wondering if God even likes them. And not only will God help you make money, but you can have a great deal of fun doing it, without all the worldly pressure. Working with God is more exciting than any adventure you've ever had before. You're going to love it!

This book is not about buying stocks and commodities, although they are mentioned; but it is mostly about letting the Holy Spirit lead you. God can lead you to money through an unlimited number of possible transactions, deals, purchases, trades, inventions, and ideas. And He'll lead you in all other decisions and endeavors as well, if you'll let Him.

So before you say, "But Bruce, I don't have any money to buy stocks, or even know how; and aren't stocks and commodities unsafe?" Please keep reading. There are many other ways to make money and this book will FILL YOU with faith, know how, and ideas! Over the years, the Holy Spirit has shown me a number of profitable opportunities from real estate, stocks, and commodities, to used cars, boats, retail merchandise, and plain ole yard sale stuff. Plus, He can show you how to get the capital needed for starting your journey. It's not that difficult.

God knows where the "deals" are, from big to small, and He knows the future. You may laugh at this, but I remember one time as I picked up a half gallon of orange juice from the grocery shelf, the Holy Spirit quietly spoke to me and said, "It's cheaper around the corner." Well, sure enough, I looked around the corner of the isle and there was a display of orange juice at a substantially reduced price. So, I bought two instead of one.

The OJ wasn't a big money making transaction, but I appreciated God caring about the small things too, and loving me enough to say something. But, He knows where the "big deals" are, as well. Many of the opportunities God has shown me have required little or no money, and sometimes, little or no risk. I know that sounds like a TV infomercial, but it's true. One of things I've learned about God is, if it's not a tremendously "good deal," it may not be from Him.

At the very least, though, you'll learn how to ignore the Recession and win at what you're doing now, and it won't be nearly as hard as you think. The first step is to simply stop joining in on always talking about the dumb economy. What good does that do? God is not depressed, and you shouldn't be either. If things get so terrible that no one has a job, and that could happen with the crazy government we have right now, God can make a bunny rabbit run right through your front door and jump into the cook-pot, so QUIT WORRYING! He'd rather that we just start listening to Him now, so that it doesn't come to that.

A little spiritual tip for you, too: Not only does He know about orange juice, but He also knows who's ready for the gospel, and where the ripe souls are. This is the true eternal wealth and it is way more important than money. Do you keep your eyes open and your antenna up for the souls that God wants to save? He'll point out the ones who are open and ready if you'll listen. In this book, we're going to learn how to pay attention to the Holy Spirit. Hearing Him is an incredible gift that should never be taken for granted.

I've often heard Christians ask, "Where are all the miracles, now?" Well, they're usually right in the middle of the things we're afraid to try, or do. God is willing, but we're often too cowardly to try anything, or get in the middle of a situation that requires a miracle.

In England, while riding home one Wednesday evening through little town called Tetbury, God prompted me and another fellow to stop and pass out tracts to a large group of young people who were hanging out in the town square. We both had the same impression, only we were tired and we wanted to keep driving. But, after a minute or two of consideration, we were sure it was God and we parked the car. Such leadings can easily be, and often are, overlooked. Then everyone loses.

To make a long story short, this crowd, mostly consisting of atheists, aggressively resisted us on everything we had to say, for the better part of an hour. After we had repeatedly said everything we could think to say to this group, with seemingly no success, I said to my friend, "I think it's time to kick the dust off our shoes; these guys are starting to get hostile." But then, just as we were starting to walk away, one young man came forth and asked, "Okay, if Jesus is real, will he heal me?" (Let me assure you, though you and I might get nervous, God is never afraid of such a challenge, and even welcomes such an opportunity.)

When that young man asked this, he actually had hope in his eyes, even though he also had a bit of an attitude, as did the whole crowd. But, the crowd's rebellious attitude didn't stop God's love. Immediately, when the young man asked about healing, the Holy Spirit's overwhelming power came over me like a blanket. From that moment on, it was no longer "Bruce" doing the talking. I felt like Clark Kent after jumping out of the phone booth.

This experience was one of the best feelings I've ever had in my life. God's power was surging through my body and there was no such thing as any doubt in my mind, whatsoever. When you have God's power on you in that measure, your usual earthly thinking disappears. I knew that boy was going to be healed no matter what happened next, whether he wanted it or not. Nothing was going to stop it.

I laid hands on him as the Bible instructs, and while the others were laughing and even mocking, God's power knocked him back and healed him instantly. He immediately started proclaiming that God's power had healed him. Then, after the young man had convinced the others that he was healed, God instantly healed two others right in front of everyone's atheistic eyes (about 40 people). With that demonstration of God's love, the whole crowd wanted to be saved and prayed a mass prayer with us, confessing Jesus as Lord.

That one little situation, which was almost overlooked, started a small revival in that community with many of the young people showing up and bringing new friends to our services in another nearby town. Looking back, I wish I had stayed a while because it might have really grown into something big with the right oversight. But, the small mindedness of the somewhat "religious" churches we were working with, kept them from running with the ball. They even seemed to resent some of the tattooed, pierced, young people who were coming into their "precious" buildings. What a shame. I've been to many churches that seem to be doing everything they can to remain small. I don't get it.

The moral of the above story is this: God knows where the souls are, and the miracles are in the places most Christians are afraid of. Please note that God's power didn't come on me when I was in the hotel room before we went out that night. And it didn't come on me in the car as we were driving, or even when we were walking toward the crowd. It came right when it was needed, which wouldn't have happened if we hadn't had enough courage to at least get in the middle of that situation in the first place. "No guts, no glory;" as the saying goes.

There would be no story to tell, no salvations, and no healings for those guys to testify about for years to come, if we had just kept driving by as most Christians would have done. Were we absolutely fearless walking toward those young people? NO, not at all! But, courage does what fear tries to stop. If there was no fear, we wouldn't need courage. But, you will grow bolder, and less fearful, with experience. Very few "bold" Christians started out bold. They "grew bold" with every tract they handed out, and every small bit of experience they lived through.

I never gave an oral report in school because I was terrified of public speaking. Maybe you can relate. But now I speak publicly on a regular basis, and I never even think about it anymore. In fact, I love it. Why? Because I got used to it and the fear went away. Plus, God always shows up to help me. Experience brings boldness, so if you're afraid of something, start small and overcome it. Start passing out gospel tracts, and before you know it, you'll be talking to people, or even preaching and doing miracles.

God also knows where the financial deals can be found, too, and how to take advantage. So don't blame Him if you are not experiencing God's power and provision. **Start believing, looking, listening, and acting.** God is certainly willing, and He even looks forward to helping you. God is love, and He thrives on blessing people. Money is everywhere; you just have to find it.

CHAPTER 1

WET YOUR APPETITE

HAVE YOU EVER ALLOWED God to show you how to make money? The Holy Spirit once led me over a thousand miles to buy a piece of property. I was apprehensive, but I found out that He certainly knows what He's doing. Are you willing to follow the Holy Spirit a thousand miles? Would you go that far when you're not sure why, or what's going to happen next? Do you have real faith and a desire for adventure, or are you always going to "play it safe?" There's a big difference between foolishness, and courageous faith. Our knowledge, coupled with our ability to hear God, will determine which of these is guiding us when we try something new and daring.

Was the thousand miles of travel worth it? Well, after living in the single home property for a couple of years (which included several acres), building erupted all around it and the Lord told me to sell it. And, unknown to me at the time, this happened to be at the peak of the current real estate boom. God's timing was perfect and I netted a tax free profit of over $430,000 from an investment made with only $10,000 down. That almost sounds like one of those "How to get rich in real estate" commercials, doesn't it?

Well, this time it's absolutely true and much more is possible with God. Do you think God is able to do something like that with you? Do you have the courage to find out? I wish I could do the same deal every year, but there's always something new that God can lead us to.

After selling that property, home values immediately began to fall drastically, so it pays to be versatile and obedient to God without hesitation. Some time later, I ran into one of the board members of the corporation that bought the property. He said to me, "Boy, you sure got lucky on the timing of that sale; it's not worth nearly as much now."

1

So I replied, "No, I wasn't lucky; I just followed God's leading and I really had no idea what was going to happen next. Luck had nothing to do with it."

There's an old saying that goes, "When preparation meets opportunity, good luck happens." Well, I don't like to use the word "luck" due to its origin, but, "good blessings" definitely happen when you're prepared and listening to God. The problem with most Christians, though, is they're not prepared and they wouldn't know what to do if God did show them something. They often don't even recognize opportunities because they're not looking. We'll have more on this later.

How about a smaller sample of God's leading, and blessing? I was driving down U.S. 1, in south Florida, when God drew my attention to a BMW convertible sitting on a used car lot. After a while, you'll start to recognize leadings from the Holy Spirit, and as with anything else, practice can make you better at this. Just try to make all your mistakes with the small things. Learn from your mistakes, but don't quit. The Holy Spirit doesn't make mistakes, but we might. Sometimes, we hear amiss, but you can get better at this with practice.

Anyway, this seemed like a Holy Spirit encounter, so I pulled into the car lot to check out the price. How could I tell this was from the Holy Spirit? Well, everything about this whole encounter had a very positive joy and excitement about it, as if God was having fun on the inside of me. That's the best way I can describe it. Due to having religion instead of a relationship, many don't know that the Holy Spirit is usually a very happy person, and He has fun blessing us. So, who am I to stop Him?

Also, I have learned to be careful about not conjuring up such a feeling on my own. Wishful thinking can be very dangerous. This is a very important key with following God, because He often uses our feelings and emotions, and you don't want them clouded with your own agenda, misleading thoughts, greed, or fear. Every con-man works off of greed and fear, and Satan does too.

Well, the salesman/owner showed me the book value of $9,000, which I normally wouldn't trust unless I looked it up myself, but I had a good feeling about this. He then said, "I'll take $6,500 for it," which surprised me because the car was in mint condition. I was cautious, but I felt I should do it, so I gave him a deposit and immediately signed the

Making Money With God

papers. Normally, I would recommend extreme caution for something that "sounds" so good, but I've learned to tell when God is warning me, and He wasn't.

Within minutes, before I could leave, someone else tried to offer the salesman more money for the car, but it belonged to me now. I drove it for a little while, and then someone offered me $10,900 for it, so I took it. I found out later that the dealer was in serious tax trouble, and he needed to sell a number of cars very fast.

Did you make a $4,000 profit on the last used car you owned? It pays to follow the Holy Spirit. I didn't know that the car was going to be such a good deal, but God did, and He's inside me looking through my eyes. He's looking through yours too, if you're saved.

Some time after that, another Christian, who read about the car in one of my other books, and admittedly lives hand to mouth most of the time, accused me of taking advantage of the BMW seller. With pride, he said, "I would have helped the guy instead of buying the car so cheap." Listen, the price of every item for sale on the planet is set for the certain reason of obtaining cash for one reason or another. And although I believe in negotiating, he was the one that offered the car at $6,500. I didn't know he was in need of tax money until later, and on top of all that, the Holy Spirit **LEAD** me to that car; and I know when God is leading me.

I think I helped that man (a dealer who was not emotionally attached to the car) a whole lot more than my broke accuser friend could have. And who knows what this car dealer was doing with his life and money, anyway. If a house is marked down from $300,000 to $250,000, do you think my "holier than thou" friend would pay the full price, just to "help out" the sellers? Christians are usually great at inaccurately judging others, but seldom experts at taking care of their own lives.

On the other hand, though, if your conscience is bothering you about such a deal, don't do it. Mine wasn't, and I would rather follow God's leading because we seldom know all the facts. There's no substitute for following the Holy Spirit.

I like to help people too, but I do it by God's leading because He knows who should get the help. When we don't know all the facts, and even if we do, it's not our business to offer our opinions about someone else's life or business, unless God is leading us for some productive reason. Try fixing yourself, first; and even then, hold your tongue unless God leads.

Sometimes, God will add His thoughts to ours. **Isn't that great? This is the same "person" who gave Solomon all of his wisdom, made Abraham wealthy through business and trading, warned Joseph of the coming famine, and led Jesus, too!** Don't let stale religion rob you of this reality. The Holy Spirit can be with you as well. Wouldn't like to have God helping you think?

Get to know Him. There's way more available to you than just reading about the fun that the guys in the Bible got to have, or just teaching about the Bible but never really experiencing anything. We have the same Holy Spirit they had, and He's not old, or weak. We have the same Spirit that empowered Christ in raising the dead, so why are you worried?

You can't retire on $4,000, but what if you did that every week, or just once a month? What if you could do it everyday? How would you like to have $4,000 in your pocket right now? Please realize that there are tremendous money opportunities everywhere. The whole world is like a giant yard sale, and the low-priced stuff you can buy today, might be a treasure to someone else tomorrow, or even immediately. The guy who bought my BMW was happy to pay beyond the book price because he wanted the car.

Stocks, commodities, houses, cars, boats, merchandise, businesses, or anything else you can think of, are selling at yard sale prices, somewhere, at some time. You just have to find them; or I should say, let God find them and then show you where they are. I have bought many cars at God's leading, and other items, just to flip for a profit. You can flip many of these items within 24 hours.

Simply for the purpose of resale, I bought a Dodge Ram pick up truck one afternoon. After praying, I spotted the truck in a parking lot while I was having lunch across the street. I made a very low offer which was accepted, and a few days later while having dinner with some friends, some fellow called me on my cell phone wanting to buy the truck. So, with our friends along for the ride, we all went to meet this guy and he handed me the agreed price, in cash, and I gave him the title. We then headed back out for dessert, which I gladly paid for out of my $1,500 profit. I had about two hours invested in the whole transaction, and though it was not exactly what I would call "a home run," it was well worth the trouble. It pays to let God lead you.

I had no way of knowing about the potential profit on that house a thousand miles away, but God knew. He probably couldn't get any of the local Christians to break their routines and go take a look at it. Maybe they were all too busy praying for a "financial breakthrough." Maybe they were working hard to make themselves trustworthy enough for God's future blessings. Or, maybe they thought that property would never increase in value. But, God knew that a very nice housing development would soon be built all around that property, tripling the value.

I'm so glad He told me about it. When God tells me to buy something, I try not to hesitate. I've missed out on some great opportunities by hesitating, as I'm sure you have. He's always led me into profit, just as He promised in His Word.

Most Christians aren't willing to follow God this way, or brave enough to take such a chance. They always want to run back to "the familiar (Egypt)," even as bad as it was, or is. They talk themselves out of possible opportunities with some good ole "human wisdom," and a bunch of reasons why it might not work. Too many of us are happy to remain in our mediocre, never walk on the water, lives. But, for the few who are willing to learn about the Holy Spirit, and follow His lead, there are plenty of adventures out there.

Most Christians are fearful of soul-winning, as well. They don't know the joy of leading someone to Christ, or experiencing a real miracle. They just don't have the courage to get in the middle of someone else's need(s), or the compassion.

Financial opportunities are even as close as your computer, or telephone. I like trading commodities and stocks because I can do it right from my notebook computer, wherever I am; and I don't have to deal with a salesman. I don't mind salesmen as long as they keep quiet, but they never do. When I trade on line, it's just me and the Holy Spirit. I don't even have to get dressed, and I don't have to talk to the potential buyers. I just key in the order and it's done in seconds, or sometimes I call the orders in on the phone.

Have you ever bought 100 ounces of gold before going to bed for the night, and then sold it in the morning because it went up $10 per ounce while you were sleeping? I have, and it's a great way to start the day.

I remember taking my family on vacation to the California coast several years ago. I had accumulated enough airline points to fly all of us free, roundtrip, from our home in Kentucky, to California. We flew into San Francisco, toured the coast for two weeks down to San Diego, and flew back from there. At God's leading, I had placed an order for some gold and soybean futures before we left. I also placed "target" orders, and "stop loss" protection orders, so I could just forget about it, and we left for California.

Well, just a couple of days after we arrived, both markets went up (as God knew beforehand) and hit my targets. So, while on vacation, our whole trip was fully paid for, and then some. I didn't watch the markets or even know what was happening. It moved without me worrying over it and my broker called to tell me that my "orders" had been filled. What a relaxing way to go on vacation, without worrying about how much you're spending or what you're missing out on at work. It's nice to have your money working for you, instead of you working for it. I think God intended that we all live this way, without worry and stress.

Listen, **God has no intention of participating in any recession, present or future, and you don't have to either!** Only those who are dependent upon others are severely affected by the troubles of a recession. You won't be laid off if you work for God, or yourself. Let God make you independent (God-sufficient), in need of nothing, as Paul taught in II Cor. 9:8. He has promised to provide for us even during a famine! Psalm 33: 18 & 19. Recessions come and go, and as governments either cause them, or make them worse, God remains the same and there'll be no lack for those who learn to hear Him. Psalm 23 wasn't written just so we would have something nice to say at funerals. What David wrote is true.

Actually, hard times can produce some pretty amazing financial opportunities. Again, Joseph became very rich during a famine, but if you're depressed and caught up in all the negative "news," you'll only miss money making opportunities and suffer right along with everyone else. The Christian life is governed by faith, or the lack thereof, and you'll eat the fruit of your beliefs whether good or bad, Prov. 18: 20 & 21. It does matter what you believe, because that is what you'll be saying with your mouth while setting your course, according to James 3:4.

If I can talk to someone for about 5 minutes, I can usually tell if the person really has faith, and probably even know what type of church he

Making Money With God

or she attends. How can I do this? It's simple: What they ***really*** believe, or don't believe, will unconsciously come out of their mouth, and this is what they'll harvest in life. Did you ever notice that people who are often sick are always talking about it?

I suggest that you determine to put all negative thinking and speaking away from you. You should guard your ears from the news casters because they are only there to sell advertising, and they do this by making every bit information sound way worse than it is. This, in turn, actually makes things become worse, due to fear.

They won't simply say that the DOW was "down" today. Instead, they will say, "The DOW JONES average ***PLUNGED*** today," even if it only dropped 100 points. They can make you feel like you might as well just give up and go get drunk. I haven't listened to the regular news since the last election. Who needs it? They seldom report the real cause of news and as far as the financial markets go, they are usually at least a month behind what's really happening. They'll still be talking about "surging oil prices" weeks after it has actually made a turn to the south.

Plus, most of the main stream news has a left-winged, anti-God bias, and they certainly don't support capitalism. Listen to those who report the truth, which certainly won't be the socialists of the liberal news media. Socialism is always promoted with "half truths," and its reprobate supporters push their favorite politicians by not telling the whole story. If the people new everything there was to know about socialism, they would never support it; hence, they must be duped.

If you want to know the end result of socialism, look at the American Indian reservations with over 80% unemployment, alcoholism, depression, no self esteem, and everyone waiting for a welfare check. Or look at Europe with their extremely high taxes and their extremely dangerous economies, as ours is becoming, too. Socialist leaders always want "a little more," and they're never satisfied, even until everything collapses. People are rioting in the streets in Europe because their socialist governments are now forced to cut benefits that the people never should have been addicted to in the first place. Is that what you want for your country? Just keep accepting socialism and it will happen.

Always remember: The government "owns" whoever it feeds, and the government doesn't "produce" anything; it only takes. And let's not forget the harshest possible end of socialism is full blown communism and total allegiance to "the State," which usually leads to the "elimination" of dissenters.

Socialism is always a wealth killer because it kills incentive. History has proven this time and time again, but there's always a new generation of foolish idealists who are willing to try it again. Free government benefits ARE NEVER really "free." In fact, they're usually way more expensive due to waste and corruption. In reality, government is only another "middle man" who is taking a percentage and driving up the cost of whatever service they're offering, which could have been obtained through the private sector with much more efficiency.

Any nation that has 50% or less of their people pulling 100% of the cart, with everyone else riding in the cart, will fail. Any business man knows this, but politicians never seem to know this. They are often like children who don't know that there is an end to their parent's money.

Ben Franklin once said, *"I am for doing good to the poor, but...I think the best way of doing good to the poor, is not making them easy in poverty, but leading or driving them out of it. I observed...that the more public provisions were made for the poor, the less they provided for themselves, **and of course became poorer.** And, on the contrary, the less was done for them, the more they did for themselves, and became richer."*

In case you don't know, Capitalism (buying, selling, and trading for a profit) is a God approved system found throughout the Bible. It is how God made Abraham and many others rich, and even Jesus endorsed it with His parable of trading the talents (capital) for a profit. The Apostle Paul also said, "Those who don't work (the able ones) shouldn't eat." People are not equal, as Jesus pointed out in the parable of the talents, and it is foolish to think that government can make them equal. But, Capitalism is a way that every man can make something of himself, according to his own ability. Capitalism and God's blessing made America the greatest nation in the world because it allows freedom of ideas, and it rewards our efforts.

We should have equal opportunity, but not by force, or by stealing from some to give to others. You can call it "redistribution of wealth," but it's still stealing. Renaming something doesn't make it okay, though we do this with many sins. When a bank robber or a burglar steals, aren't they just trying to "redistribute wealth?"

There are many in our society now who want us to believe that

Making Money With God

capitalism is evil, and the cause of all our social ills. They want to destroy all freedom and bring us under their heavy hand of control. They use very deceptive terms such as, "social justice, fairness, equality, and a level playing field." Don't those words sound fair and righteous? In reality, these terms simply mean taking property and money from those who have earned it, and giving it to those who have not. This is simply a means to control thought, beliefs, and wealth, which is power. "Soviet justice" would be a more appropriate term. This evil philosophy has even crept into some churches.

Sure we should help the poor, but not by making slaves out of the workers, or through stealing the wealth of others through a "middleman" government that's taking the lion's share. Less government is the best thing for any country; otherwise, evil will always prevail.

The huge lie behind all this "social justice" thinking is: "If someone is rich, they're causing others to be poor, or taking their share." Only those who don't understand the creation of wealth will think and agree with such foolishness. Wealthy people are usually busy making others wealthy and prosperous, too. If you're poor, it's not because someone else is rich. It's because you don't think right. Punish the rich for being rich, and everyone will become poor, which is what the Socialists really want because rich people are hard to control.

Wealth can be "created," so there is never a limited supply that must be divided by totalitarians. There's enough wealth in this world for everyone to be rich, but people must be taught how to gain on their own. Give it to them through socialism, and it will soon disappear. The answer is "training people," and if they won't be trained, there's nothing you can do for them. Handouts are temporary.

Don't let your Christian friends be negative. I know Christians who just constantly talk about the "bad economy," and as a result, their personal lives are immersed in the "bad fruit" of their own words. They live in fear and worry just like those who don't know God. We should focus on God's promises, not those of the doom and gloom pundits. I've had some people actually get angry with me because I mentioned that we shouldn't be extremely affected by the economy. We should decide we're not going to participate in the recession, but some Christians are right in the middle of it because on their own mouths.

Why don't you come into the light and start working with God? He's NOT fearful, confused, or wondering what to do next! Listen, faith is found in two places, and two places only. It is found in the heart, and in the mouth. And if it's not coming out of your mouth, it's not in your heart. If worry about the economy is all that's coming out of your mouth, then faith in God's provision is not real to you because it hasn't been planted in your heart. It doesn't matter what you're careful to say at church when you know others are listening. Your life will be ruled by what's coming out of your mouth all day long, every day. And what ever is coming out of your mouth regularly, is what's really in your heart.

A "recession" is nothing more than a slowdown in spending, usually triggered by bad news and fear. Then the fear can actually produce the negative things that weren't even real, at first. I hope you understand that, because fear is a negative form of faith and it can produce evil, just like faith can produce good things. It is imperative that you get fear out of your life and start taking control of your life with confidence.

The economy is like the tide; it comes in, and it goes out. This has always happened and it always will. Sometimes the tide just happens to go out farther than usual, but that doesn't mean that the whole ocean has disappeared. God is not nervous about the economy, and we shouldn't be either. We must believe that He'll make a distinction between us and the world, as He did between Israel and Egypt. When Israel was right with God, they had "no lack," even during some very bad times.

If you keep listening to the television, you'll start believing that the whole ocean has dried up, even though there's still plenty of business going on. If you belong to God, you should be getting the best of it. If you trust God, customers and clients will call you before anyone else, because you have God's **favor**. This is a Biblical fact, and it should be working for you. If this isn't happening, you need to examine what's coming out of your mouth, continuously. Are you thanking God for favor, or are you complaining about the economy and your circumstances? Let God make you an example of His love to those around you. Don't stop the flow by being fearful, negative, and full of doubt.

Let me say a little about God's favor on your life. I've heard many sermons on how to get God's favor; you know, the "seven steps to this or that" kind of stuff. And most all of the sermons I've heard on favor, even in the most popular churches, were legalistic and erroneous, even though they "sounded" good. It seems we just love to hear legalistic

Making Money With God

stuff because we like following steps one, two, and three, instead of developing real faith.

Ask yourself this; "Does a child immediately have the parent's favor when the child is born, even though the child hasn't done a thing to earn it?" WELL OF COURSE IT DOES! And you have God's favor as soon as you're "born again" into His family, without lifting a finger. Please forget all the "How to obtain God's favor" junk, and start believing that you really are "IN CHRIST!" Do you believe that Jesus has God's favor? Then so do you if you're "in Him!" Start speaking about the favor of God on your life, now, instead of magnifying your problems with a mouth full of doubt. Christians have authority in this world, and because of this, demons can, and will, use what *you say* against you, if it's contrary to God's promise. You can learn more about this in my book on "faith."

Although we all may fail from time to time, we (YOU) were not created for failure, depression, fear, or despair. You weren't made to be kicked around by circumstances, or to be ruled over by others who seem to have the upper hand! And God is NOT doing this to you to make you a better person. **You were made to RULE AND REIGN!** You were made for faith, power, abundance, dominion, authority, and joy! All of these things are realized by changing the way you think! Do you know that along with Jesus, you too are a son of God, and a king?

Do you know that God loves you as much as He loves Jesus? Jesus said this with His own mouth in John 17:23. That would be a very good place to start renewing your mind. Start believing that YOU ARE a son and heir of God Almighty! It's your mind, and your beliefs are simply the result of choice. So choose LIFE! Stop believing that you're only some sort of "servant/steward" who hopefully, will be "good enough" to be a son, someday! BELIEVE you're a son NOW! I know that most of the church teaches the "you're an unworthy servant" mentality, but that is NOT what God thinks about you! He believes you're family.

So what now? Well, let the renewing your mind continue, and may you start walking as a king, today. Let's break free from the "someday" thinking that most Christians are in bondage to, and start enjoying God's grace and blessings NOW! God has already approved of us and said "yes" to every promise (II Cor. 1:20), so we simply need to learn how to "possess the land."

If you've received Jesus and have been washed in the blood of Christ, you qualify for everything God has, **right now,** including wisdom for wealth, and inside information from the Holy Ghost. And you will always be qualified for this information as long as you're "IN HIM!" So, once again, stop thinking "I must prove myself and be good enough for *someday."* You are God's very own righteousness, NOW!" II Cor. 5:21 You can't get any more righteous than that!

We're not on probation for our past sins, and we have nothing to prove to anyone, especially God. So you can start having faith right now! "Today is the day of salvation!" If you're trapped in some sort of "merit badge, prove yourself gospel," this book will be a tremendous blessing to you.

The reason God gives us wealth, is **because He has wealth, and we belong to Him, PERIOD**. This is a Biblical fact.

Most Christians can't accept this simple truth, though. They've been taught for years (not by God) that God won't bless anyone until they've run the gauntlet of God's imaginative and numerous tests, which God and everyone else already knows, you'll probably fail. (That's kind of why He sent Jesus, instead of you.) But, the church keeps on saying "amen" to such teaching even though our teachers, who started way before us, haven't seemed to have passed the barrage of tests, either.

If the above "reason God gives us wealth" is too simple for your religious head, then go ahead and practice your "not quite good enough, religious stair climbing." You can climb to "the next level" for years if you like. And when you finally realize you're not getting anywhere because you're trying to climb "up" the "down" escalator (your works), then come back and see us.

After you're completely worn out from working all your "heaven opening," legalistic systems, to open a heaven that Jesus has ALREADY opened, maybe you'll finally listen and learn that everything we receive from God is by **GRACE**, and through faith, only. Maybe you'll finally believe He's already said "YES" to all His promises (II Cor. 1:20), and that you're already "seated in a heavenly place with Christ (Eph. 2:6)." That is the highest possible "level" available, and you're already there!

If you haven't received Jesus (been born again) yet, than do it now by simply asking Jesus to save you and by confessing Him as your Lord. This is how you become part of God's family and gain access to everything He has, according to Romans chapter 10. Believe me, you're

Making Money With God

present life will be much better if you'll make Jesus the Lord of your life, not to mention your life in eternity.

Also, if you're new to Christianity and unfamiliar with the Holy Spirit, or His gifts and leadings, I want to mention that we're not talking about anything that has to do with psychics, mediums, fortune tellers, readings, astrology, communing with the dead, spiritualism, or any such thing. Those things are all demonic in nature (even if they talk about God). They are simply demonic counterfeits of the real gifts of the Spirit taught in I Corinthians, chapter 12.

Stay away from such things and seek God through Jesus only. With time, you'll be able to detect the fake stuff. No one who is truly "speaking for God" will be charging money for their "prophecies," and there are other ways to tell who's real. Study the Word (especially the New Testament) and stay in a good church. Soon, you'll be able to discern who's of God, who's of the devil, who's wrong, and who's fake. How can you tell if it's a good church? Does the pastor(s) love Jesus, people, and the Bible; and is the Holy Spirit there? Just because it's called a church, doesn't necessarily mean it's endorsed by God.

Churches are like restaurants. Some have really good food, but most don't. I've been to many churches that have great music, talented speakers, wonderful programs, but no presence of God. My feeling is; if God doesn't attend, why would I want to? We should be choosey.

CHAPTER 2

QUALIFICATIONS

MONEY, IT'S SOMETHING THAT seems so very hard for some of us to get our hands on. I know what that feels like. But then there are others who just seem to walk outside and pick it up off the ground. Why is that? Why is it so easy for some, and so hard for others? What do the money makers know, that the wannabes don't?

Someone very close to me recently said, "After years of going to school, I finally have my Master's Degree, but I still don't know *how to make money.*" I've really given that statement a lot of thought, and I wonder how many others need to realize that this is their problem, too? After all, most of our education systems don't really teach us how to make money. They usually only teach us skills that will hopefully get us hired, which is a start, but it falls way short of what we really need to know. And most people eventually realize that working for someone else isn't going to fulfill their dreams.

Sooner or later, and even in the midst of a satisfying career, most people turn their attention to having more money. When we're young, we don't expect too much, so we don't think much about making more as we assume that more money will come with age and hard work. After all, that's "fair" isn't it? Unfortunately, though, this is not automatic. Usually, when you're working for someone else, most of your effort goes toward making them rich, and not you. Usually, hard work without wisdom only produces sweat. But on the other hand, wisdom without hard work might only produce disappointment. Put them together, though, and it's like mixing nitro with glycerin.

Even those who have well paying jobs have to put their money in places where, hopefully, it will turn into more. This may be for retirement, children, education, security, or just plain ole fun, but

Making Money With God

eventually, most of us would like for our money to work for us, instead of us working for it. But, will we know how?

For many of our predecessors of the previous 60 – 80 years, the assumption was; "if I do everything according to conventional saving and investing rules, I will be okay." But recent years have shown us that fairness, good intentions, and traditional investing, can be pretty unreliable. We've found that only one bad election can cripple the wealth of a whole country. Today's savvy investor must know what's going to happen, good or bad, before it happens.

Someone once said, and it's true: "Every dollar you have, or can access for use, is a soldier at your command." Soldiers need to be strategically placed for best use, and with this in mind, we can no longer be lazy or trust other people with our money. We must act as if we're in a war, and many enemies, including our own governments, are trying to find, and take, our money. Knowing this, it may be necessary to move our troops (money), more quickly, and more often, than in years gone by. For this type of warfare, it is a great advantage if we can stay in touch with God. And if you don't have any money to "move," well, God can also show you how to get some.

Do you remember the Bible story where God's army was able to know every move their enemy was making? This was because God was revealing it through someone who was in constant communication with God. (II Kings 6:8-12) With "foreknowledge," God's army was able to "ambush the ambush." What a great advantage that was, bringing God's people a great victory. But, today, anyone who comes to Jesus can be filled with the same Holy Spirit that made that story possible. We have no excuse for failure, and even if we do make mistakes, or "blow it," sooner of later we will come out on top if we don't give up.

How much better would it be if we started out early in life making money beyond our paychecks? Why should we wait until we lose interest in our careers, or get tired of the hard work we've been doing, when money could be working for us now? Then, if we want to pursue other careers or projects, it will be totally by choice, instead of force. Wouldn't that be nice?

And before you lose interest by thinking that I'm talking about "investing" in 401-k's, or different types of mutual funds, I'm not. We're discussing more exciting, income producing, "trades" and opportunities of all kinds; and you can start small, and immediately, if you like. You can learn about the boring, so called "safe investment" stuff, later. (Really, there's nothing "safe" unless you're listening to God.) And don't think you have to have huge sums of money to start making money, because you don't. It's true that the more you have, the easier it will be, but do you know that if you start with a penny and double your money every day for just one month, at the end of the month you will have over 5 million dollars? Go ahead, do the math.

With trading, you're not going to double your money on every transaction, but sometimes you'll do even better than that. Because it was leveraged when I sold the above property, I roughly made a 1,000 % (one thousand per cent) increase. I ended up with about 10 times the money I had invested, including what I paid to make a certain number of payments. When you make trades, if you keep your hands off your profits, it won't be very long before you can consider any type of buying and selling you'd like to do. **ALL** money making, of any kind, or any where, consists of some type of buying and selling of goods and services. It's really not that hard to figure out. It all comes down to selling something for a profit, and that means learning to buy right.

If you can't buy better than wholesale, look for something else. But, do allow for Holy Ghost exceptions to this, and all rules. A small profit is better than none. Occasionally, "buying high" is the right thing to do, especially if the item is on its way to even a higher price. Those who didn't buy Google at $100 per share probably thought it was way too expensive at $200. But, those who knew it would go to $400 per share, and higher, were glad to get it at $200. Again, the Holy Spirit knows what every stock is going to do.

But, buying high was totally wrong for those who bought real estate at the top of the 2006 boom. They didn't have God's wisdom, or leading. But right now, in January of 2010, those who knew to wait are starting to "flip" houses again and they're making profits. Impatience is very costly, and even beyond praying, there are ways to know when to buy, and when to wait. Usually, when everyone is doing it, be very afraid. But, when everyone is afraid to do it, it's probably the right time to buy. I have a rule for buying, though: If God isn't saying anything, or assuring me that I'm right, I don't do anything. Prayer and your inward witness are always the best indicators for timing, if you'll learn to recognize certain leadings.

The wisdom of knowing market patterns, which comes with

experience, is also something that is very useful. I have found that God expects me to observe the obvious. If the tide is way out, it is a given that it is going to come back in. This is true with markets as well, and when you know where the tide boundaries are, which anyone can obtain by constantly watching, God expects you to pay attention to what you know from the natural realm. Just be sure this doesn't contradict His specific leading(s), though, because sometimes in market watching, the tide might not come back on a regular schedule, and timing is everything.

People are always telling me about possible new technologies, or ideas that "might" be introduced soon. But personally, I usually don't pay much attention to investments that promise possible returns that could take years to realize. Investing like that can pay off eventually, but I like to consider things that are in place and on the verge of moving soon. Too many things can render a good idea for today, obsolete tomorrow. Due to rapidly changing technology, and/or political interference, a good business idea can disappear over night. For me, there are just too many things that can happen to the stuff that takes years to come to fruition.

It's great to be ahead of the wave, but a big piece out of the middle isn't so bad, either. We should be glad to get any part of a financial move. We don't need to brag about being the first one in, and we should always be cautious of staying too long. Someone once said, "Only a fool holds on for top dollar." This is a very good warning. Most of my mistakes have not been from picking the wrong trade, but from getting out at the wrong time. Unless you're just in for a dividend, never forget that the price moving music will surely stop, sooner or later.

Unlike shares of stocks, real estate and most commodities have pretty strict trading ranges that are going to lock in their movement to some degree. So, if we're paying attention, we should know when they're at a top or bottom, unless there's a "breakout" of their normal trading range. Then different rules apply.

Stocks have ranges too, but shares can move out of these ranges with much less effort, and go much farther. For instance; a one hundred thousand dollar home isn't going to easily become a one million dollar home (ten times the usual value). Why? Because no one in their right mind will buy it at a price that's way above other comparable homes, and banks won't loan beyond the appraisal. But, stocks are not so easy to

A. Bruce Wells

compare; and a share of stock can easily go from $10 to $100, or higher, with just a couple of ingredients and the right news.

Why does this happen? Because the value of a share of stock (a piece of paper), is often only a matter of perception, and it's much more difficult to say what it is actually worth. In reality, something is only worth what others are willing to pay. At the peak of the Dutch Tulip Mania, during the late 1630's, some single tulip bulbs literally sold for more than 10 times the annual income of a skilled craftsman. So that "worth," for a short time, was just as real as what someone would pay now for one bulb.

That 1630's price is unbelievable to us now, but such things still happen to some degree; usually because everyone gets caught up in the frenzied fear of missing out. But of course, as these things always do, the tulip market crashed much faster than it took off, and it left many investors completely wiped out because they got in late, or they held on too long.

I remember the "great silver spike" of 1980, when a couple of billionaires tried to corner the market on silver. Silver was trading at less than $5 per ounce then, but in a very short period of time, a buying frenzy took it to $50 per ounce. Those who rode it up made a great deal of money (50 dollars per penny, per contract), but those who got in late (the sheep), were probably wiped out on its sudden, huge drop, unless they "shorted" the market. You should look at the silver chart from 1980. Then you'll know what happened to tulips, and how it can happen to something else in the near future. Wouldn't it be great to know about such a move in advance? Such enormous moves are rare, but less aggressive "spikes" happen on a regular basis.

Speculators often buy into a market simply because they know everyone is excited about something, and this alone will greatly drive the price. The trick is to not be left standing when the music stops. There are always a huge numbers of people (again, the sheep) who don't consider that these buying frenzies will end, and they are left holding the proverbial "bag." But, on the other hand, there are always those savvy people (the few) who make fortunes waiting for, and betting on, the inevitable downturn of soaring markets. And whether or not it will be a soft landing, or a crash (which is determined by the amount of fear generated when everyone starts jumping ship), they still make money.

Governments are notorious for causing such melt downs, as they did

Making Money With God

with this last housing market while trying to control inflation. Of course the government guys have convinced everyone that the Capitalists, Wall Street, and the other "party," caused the economic meltdown. (Hitler blamed the Jews for Germany's problems.) But, anyone who will take the time to follow the real facts in reverse, and has an honest heart, will soon know it was the Liberal (left) Governeers who set the whole collapse in motion by forcing banks to loan money to unqualified borrowers.

This foolish legislation created the bundles of bad loans that were sold, and then resold, again and again. The rest of the story is only a trail of falling dominos. Every time a government tries to solve a problem that should be left alone, they create 10 more problems. But these same people see these new problems as opportunities for more legislation. They love this kind of stuff.

If they would just leave things alone, such markets will always correct themselves, and usually with a lot less pain. But, politicians just can't leave things alone. They must always appear to be doing something, or they might not be needed. A good policeman only has to be visible to be effective. He doesn't have to stop traffic just to show that he can, or to get the glory for fixing the problem he caused.

Economic chaos is the easiest, proven way for subversive types to gain inroads into government control. So don't be surprised when you see some politicians doing things that are obviously hurtful to the economy. They can't pass freedom robbing, power grabbing, legislation, unless there appears to be a need. I know that sounds "conspiracy minded," but it's still true.

As long as there is a free society where Christians can worship the one true God of the Bible, there will always be those, people who lean toward darkness, who will work toward ending it. They may do this knowingly, or even unknowingly, but they're certainly being used by Satan. It's the spiritual side they've chosen by default. Jesus said, "If you're not for me, you're against me." The "anti-Christ" spirit is very busy in our world, and destroying freedom would be very "progressive" for the spiritual world of darkness. The Bible says that Satan appears as an "angel of light," or a person(s) pretending to be good, and politics is where the power is.

Getting back to trading, sure, there are pricing formulas for stocks, but the person who bought at $10, may think $40 is way too high simply because it is 4 times what he or she paid. But, the person who started watching the stock at $35 might jump in when he sees the stock move higher. He or she might believe that $80 is the new target. And still yet again, another buyer might think $80 is a steal, because he's convinced it's going to $100. Any item of trade is only worth something because someone else wants it. As soon as the interest is gone, the value disappears.

I remember when Apple was $35 per share and soon went to $180. I thought this was an insanely high price, but now it's at $255. If I hadn't been watching it at $35, the $180 probably wouldn't have seemed so high. Again, perception is a major influence in stocks. If I had bought a thousand shares at $35 just a couple of years ago, which I didn't, I would be ahead at least $220,000, and probably more because I would have used the margin (credit) available from my broker. Even my wife told me to buy it, but I was too busy fooling with some other trades, so I let it pass. She reminds me of her suggestion, often.

Houses, and a number of various commodities, are much easier to track. When wheat gets too expensive, the food companies stop buying future contracts (futures), and the price comes down. If houses shoot up out of their normal range, making a bubble, eventually they'll come back down because people will stop buying what they can't afford. Those who bought real estate in 2006, did not know this, or ignored the warnings. When gas topped $4 per gallon here in South Florida, most of the pleasure boats disappeared off the water ways on Sunday afternoons, a time when they are normally packed with boats. It wasn't very long though, until the prices dropped due to a lack of demand (interest). Then the boats returned.

Again, our government foolishly set us up for the housing crash by forcing banks to loan money (that didn't belong to the banks or the government) to unqualified people. The bankers were literally threatened with jail time and huge fines if they didn't break their normal, "sensible" guidelines and loan to the unqualified. Was this unfair to the unqualified? Absolutely not! They're the ones who are mostly being foreclosed, and now they're less qualified than before! The best answer would have been to teach the "unqualified" how to qualify, if this is what they wanted. If anything, this whole plan was "unfair" to those who actually followed the rules of qualification before they were thrown in the trash.

The super-easy-to-get money triggered a buying frenzy and prices rose. Then, the Fed tried to "make" prices come down by raising interest rates, which brought everything to a sudden "stand still." They screwed things up in both directions, and have made the rest of the world suffer for their foolishness.

They could have waited for a slow, natural market correction, which would have happened soon enough, but again, politicians seldom have anything to do other than negatively interfering with the lives of normal, hardworking people. Now they're making us all pay for the foreclosures, and much more. None of this would be happening if they had just stayed out of the banking business.

This is why all congressional positions should be "volunteers" only, with term limits. When we pay lawmakers (and they're very well paid), they feel obligated to continuously make laws, and most are harmful or unnecessary. New laws usually lead to more spending and less freedom, and again, every financial problem in the world today is due to politicians spending what their countries don't have.

Politicians are usually very stupid about free markets, or profit making businesses in general. The administration we have in the U. S. now, 2010, has very few, if any, business experienced people on board. Most are just idealistic, naïve, career politicians, which is usually a recipe for wealth killing socialism. They seldom know how to create wealth. In fact, they usually don't even know where it comes from. Again, they only know how to tax it.

Successful business experience should be a legal pre-requisite for holding public office. The ones who have only schooling and political experience, usually know nothing more than how to tax, spend, and waste your money. And to make a name in history, they feel they must craft some groundbreaking new legislation, which is almost always unwanted by freedom loving Americans.

GETTING CAUGHT BY EMOTION

When trying to make decisions, many Christians think that the absence of a "red light" feeling in their spirit is the same as having a "green light" from God. But this thinking has brought many Christians into a world of financial hurt and problems, simply because they "wanted" something and they talked themselves into it, or someone else did.

God never said "okay" to their plan(s), but because He didn't stop them either, they took this as an "okay." Then later they'll say, "Well, God allowed this for a reason." This is kind of a subtle way of blaming God for their mistake, and their wishful thinking.

Well, Guess what. God "allows" almost everything; and He permits almost everything, even our dumb decisions. He allows murder, rape, wars, killing, child abuse, adultery, lies, hate, perversion, deception, and you name it; but that doesn't mean that He approves of it, or planned it. He'll also allow us to believe stupid things, and make foolish choices, like attending a dead church. But, just because He doesn't stop you, that doesn't mean that He agrees with you. It just means that you didn't seek His opinion about the situation, or listen sufficiently. God doesn't make you think the way you think, and everything that happens to you isn't by divine design, as many teach. It is foolishness to think so.

In one of my other books, I wrote of a man I knew who bought a piece of property at the wrong time, the top of the last real estate boom. He bought it and then very quickly lost more than half of his rather large investment. After he spoke about this situation, he then said, "Oh well, God is in control." Many Christians like to blindly use this phrase, but, was God really in control when he bought that property, or did he just make a bad choice?

I also tried to buy some property at the same time, in the same area, and the Holy Spirit simply would not give me a "release" to buy. In fact, I looked at one house after another for several months, but I just couldn't pull the trigger even though I saw some very good buys. I never "felt" the peace of God on anything I looked at, so I waited, and I'm so glad I did. In reality, it turned out that at that time, nothing was a "good buy" with the unforeseen housing crash on its way. I would be in the same boat with this other fellow, and countless others, if I hadn't listened to my inward witness. If the peace is gone, God is warning you. And if you can't tell one way or the other, you haven't spent enough time with God.

This other fellow may have missed God's warning due to any number of reasons. Maybe he was caught up in the fear of "missing out" on the property before it went up in price. Frenzies can produce many mistakes. I've certainly made my share.

The fear of "missing out" is a common motivation that causes a multitude of financial blunders. This fear is rooted in greed and poverty thinking, and this same thinking drives much of our advertising, and contributes to our debt mentality. Even Christian fundraising employs such tactics by making you think you're going to "miss out" on God's provision if you don't hurry up and send an offering "now." Fear is the motivation instead of faith. Financially secure people, and/or those who have a solid faith in God's steady, unfailing provision, don't fall for such tactics. They know that God's salvation is constant, and not based on emotional whims, "seasons," or so called "special releases."

Our covenant of salvation doesn't fluctuate with the calendar, special revelations, or human bursts of emotion. I wish I had a dollar for every "special move of God's provision" I tried to get in on. These "special moves," usually presented with the fervor of a carnival barker, were allegedly going to solve all my problems. But, after years of being foolish, I finally realized they were only solving the problems of the guys touting these illusive "outpourings" of God. I sent offering after offering and still remained poor. It wasn't until I started "listening" to God, and using real, raw, faith in God's total redemption by grace that I started to prosper.

During the same time period of the ill-timed property purchase above, a friend of mine wanted me to partially finance a small house he wanted to flip, and I agreed. But, then, every time I heard the phrase "sub-prime mortgages," a phrase that was brand new to everyone at the time, I got a very bad feeling about doing a house deal of any kind. So, I told my friend that I just didn't feel good about going ahead and we called the lawyer and stopped the proceedings. Well, you know the rest of the story about the "sub-primes," and we avoided a lot of trouble because the Holy Spirit was nice enough to warn me. That little house never did sell.

Always wait for God's "go ahead." Do you remember what happened to Saul when he didn't have the patience to wait for Samuel's arrival? I just gave you some huge money saving advice. You should send me a thousand dollars for what you just read. If you're impetuous or antsy, you're going to buy the wrong thing, or at the wrong time, or both; and you're going to have a lot of trouble recovering from mistakes. You must learn to wait for the opportunity and the right timing. Homerun hitters don't just walk up to the plate and swing at any pitch. They wait for "their" pitch. A loosing trade, today, might be a winner next week. Timing is everything.

Let me add one other valuable thing about timing. **NEVER, EVER,** chase a trade or a "time sensitive" opportunity; and most all ARE time sensitive. I have lost more money chasing opportunities that I was right about, but acted on late, than I would have if I had just been totally wrong about the trade. Unless you have an extremely CLEAR "word" from God, just let the opportunity go and look for the next one. These things are like surfing. If you're not ready for the wave, it will pass you by. And if you chase it, you might miss the next one, too. Remember; there's always another wave coming.

WILL CHURCH SHOW US WHAT TO DO?

Since most of our sources of education don't really train the average person in the skills of really making money, and the other common place of learning for the Christian, the church, doesn't really teach us how to make money either, what should we do? Oh sure, you'll hear many sermons on money, but most of these sermons consist of you proving your faithfulness with a varied handful of alleged Christian responsibilities. Such teaching won't actually tell you how to make money, though. Plus, many of these requirements aren't even from God. Non-Christians are out making money everywhere, simply because they know how.

But nonetheless, we're led to believe that after an unknown allotted time of probation, in which we "work" to prove ourselves "faithful," God will eventually be impressed and open heaven on us. Hopefully though, you won't be one of those who will get caught in this trap and wait 5, 10, or maybe 20 years before finally starting to seek real answers about money. Maybe you'll start now. Be sure of this; God is only impressed with your faith in His blood bought redemption, and not with the lackluster works that you "think" are proving to God that you can be trusted.

Just yesterday, I heard someone who is normally a very good Bible teacher, explain that "God *won't* bless you financially if you've abused what He's already given you and you've gone into debt with your credit cards and other various things requiring payments." Doesn't that sound sensible and true? Such thinking is often presented in many different ways, and on the surface, it sounds very reasonable. And we should be responsible, but, when we add the "God won't bless you, unless you

_____," we take money out of the grace arena and add one more thing to the ever growing list of subliminal church requirements for money. We're often led to believe that these things must be done to maintain God's "free" favor, especially in the area of money.

I believe everyone should be wise, disciplined, and responsible with their money. But, at the same time, if financial provision is part of our redemption which was paid at the cross, it is not wise to imply that God "will not bless" until everything is in order. How many times have you had to ask forgiveness for the same thing?

This same preacher would never say that the forgiveness of sins can not be obtained until "you straighten out your entire life." Most churches would never send someone home from the altar saying, "Come back after you get away from all your sinful friends, and overcome all your sinful habits, and then we'll pray with you to be saved." But, we regularly imply that this is the way it is with money.

God deals with each of us on an individual basis, and maybe in certain situations He might tell someone there are special conditions for His help in a particular situation. But, my problem is with the broad sweeping implications, and the underlying ideas, that are launched from our pulpits continuously reinforcing the "You must prove your worthiness and earn God's trust before God will bless you" philosophy. These ideas are rampant in the church world when it comes to money, as if they're actually doctrinal; but they are not.

You will have much more success learning to trust God, instead of trying to get Him to trust you. God is much smarter than that. Did the prodigal son get to "prove" his trustworthiness as a servant? After blowing all of his money, did he have to prove he could now handle money before gaining access to the father's provision? The answer is, NO! The father (God) accepted him instantly, and reinstated his position as "heir." Believe me; everyone already knows you can't be trusted. How do we know this? We know because you're as flaky as the rest of us, and we can't be trusted either. But, God CAN BE trusted, every time.

I'm not advocating irresponsibility, but there are so many rules and regulations presented to Christians concerning money, that somebody has to say something. I've gotten financial miracles when I deserved them the least, and maybe you have to, so why is it that the church has built a never ending labyrinth of obstacles that must be overcome before God will give us a few dollars? Abraham's entire line was blessed because of one promise made to Abraham. Sometimes, it seems that even the Old Covenant was easier than what much of the church teaches.

Sure, there are some really fine, Bible teaching men of God out there doing great things for God, but it is just not very likely that you'll actually hear the financial stuff that really works. It's just not the main focus of church, and rightfully so. When it comes to money, the church is almost entirely "works" minded. This situation needs correcting, but it's not very likely to happen. Much of the so called "gospel" in today's church, is really some kind of performance agenda designed to convince God to give us what He's already freely given (Romans 8:32). And no one ever seems to tell us when we've gotten passed the qualification point, or that God has already said, "Okay, you're approved."

Financial help and wisdom from God should be as free as forgiveness, but it's never presented that way, even though it is part of redemption. Many Christians literally spend years (like I did) listening to grace-coated legalism that's inadvertently disguised as "obedience, faithfulness, or doing the Word." And the only thing that's reaped from such preaching is little more than a feeling of disqualification, or a determination to do better, which only brings frustration to those who are trying so hard to meet the grade. Or, there are those who are full of pride because they think they actually *are* meeting the grade.

We attend church faithfully, take reams of notes, buy cases of recorded sermons, go to conference after conference, and like my friend with the Master's Degree, we still don't know how to make money. But, we're hoping God will "honor" all of our hard work(s), and send us a check. And to keep us from giving up, week after week we're told that the "payoff" will eventually come to the faithful few, "someday."

Then when God does bless someone due to His love, prayer, grace, and adoption; the credit goes to their works when they're called on to testify. We just can't seem to get to the place where we really believe in grace, and free salvation. But, if you ever do come to the understanding of our real grace based salvation, it will feel like walking out of a cave into the sunlight. You'll finally understand the "peace" that Jesus spoke of, and the joy that Paul had in prison.

Most of today's Christians would have been in that prison going over their checklist, beating their heads against the bars while trying to figure out what they did wrong. "Why is God punishing me?" "What did I do to deserve this?" A million questions would be on their lips,

Making Money With God

instead the praise that will shake the doors open. Bewilderment and questions are all you have when you've been taught so many spiritual formulas that you can't even keep track. They're supposed to bring a certain result for a certain action, but they just don't. That's because they're works, and not faith based on grace.

For years, I taught such things myself. Then one evening, as I was preparing for a service in Hannibal, MO, the Holy Spirit visited me in a hotel room. That visit (you can read about it in my other book) changed my life and ministry, drastically. Now I'm a stickler for only that which is true, real, proven, and what God actually intended. There's just not a whole lot of that in church, although most ministers think they have a handle on truth, as I did before that special visitation.

Of course, before Hannibal, I would have said I was preaching only the truth, as most ministers would now, but God revealed that I wasn't. I just accepted the same ole "someday" cliché reasoning that everyone around me embraced. Like many others, I was using "out of context" verses to prove *"my"* point, instead of trying to discover what God was really saying in those verses. Brutal honesty with your self will work wonders. I'm amazed at the number of fruitless, kicked around financial clichés I still hear taught in many churches as the gospel. Such teaching has become epidemic in magnitude.

Forgive me for belaboring this point, but there's a much easier way to be blessed by God than the way we've been taught. I wasted 12 years listening to "how to open heaven" sermons, and "the keys to releasing God's blessings" sermons, and "how to get God's financial favor" sermons, from ministers who meant well, but really had no clue. No one ever bothered to point out that Jesus had already **totally opened heaven, purchased our total acceptance, earned our total approval, and because we're "in Him," we're granted a total YES to all of God's promises!** And this has been true for all New Testament believers for over 2,000 years.

Again, the church teaches this good news for the forgiveness of sins, but not for financial provision. In the financial realm, we (the church) thinks that the Bible actually says, "We're saved by "works," through sweat, and not by grace; for this is the *Law* of the church, and God won't give you anything until you prove you deserve it." 1st Confusion 2:8. Of course that verse isn't really in the New Testament, but it's still taught quite regularly, only it's not so obvious.

In my first years of going to church, no one seemed to know that heaven was already opened, and they still don't. Everywhere I went for answers, they were teaching "how to open heaven," and everyone else was trying to figure out why it wasn't working for them. Finally, after much prayer, the Holy Spirit had mercy on me and explained to me from John 1: 51, and again from II Cor. 1:20, that **heaven is already open on those who are "in Christ!"**

God, Himself, had to show me that I was totally wasting my time and energy on trying to open heaven. He did this because I was begging Him for real answers, since the church stuff didn't seem to be working for me, or anyone else I knew. At that time, I had never heard the information God gave me about heaven being open from anywhere, and everyone was working as hard as they could to pry it open. For some reason, Christians seem to love legalism, and most still are trying to open heaven. I think they just don't feel they deserve anything for free, and would prefer to earn it. That simply doesn't work with salvation, or any part of it.

Everyday there were new revelations on why our attempts to open heaven were not working. Yet, we knew if we could just "tweak things a bit," or "adjust them a little more", or "repent a little better," blessings would surely start to flow. At least this is what we were led to believe, week after week. So, we would try harder, pray longer, increase our studying, sing louder, and do more, but we never seemed to catch up to the carrot that was being dangled before us. Let me save you a huge amount of time. No one ever does.

You can keep rowing against the wind, or you can start acting like Jesus. You can keep working your formulas, or you can start listening to the Holy Spirit. The choice is yours alone, but don't think that everyone else will want to join you. Most of us love our religion and traditions way to much for any real, useful change. As long as we have enough to get by, we're not going to seek any real answers. We prefer our state of semi-sleep because truth brings responsibility.

NEWS FLASH! If you're hidden "in Christ," heaven is already open on you! I just can't say that too many times! Do you think heaven is closed on Jesus, the head of the church? How crazy would that be? So, if we are His body, it's OPEN on us, too! If we could open heaven and earn God's blessings ourselves, why would we even need Jesus?

And really, what difference does it make if heaven is open or not?

Making Money With God

God is with us here, and even inside us! This is a revelation that is still hidden from the church, even though it get's briefly mentioned from time to time on a very shallow plane. Every struggling Christian in the world wouldn't be trying so hard to reach that illusive "breakthrough," if they only knew that Christ was inside them. Most of them think He's hiding somewhere behind a cloud, until they pull the right strings, push the right buttons, and say the magic words.

I'm not trying to be all negative on the church, but I push these points strongly, and repeatedly, because "performance thinking," **will, without a doubt, interfere with your ability to follow the Holy Spirit**. Did you really hear what you just read? Go back and read it again and again!

The *"carnal mind"* ("a flesh centered mind," or literally, a mind that is focused on works, or dos & don'ts), is at enmity with the Spirit of God, according to Romans 8:7. In other words; if you're focused on your performance (accomplishments, duties, works, etc.), you'll miss God's leading, or be at odds with Him as you remind Him of your amazing and stellar Christian behavior.

Also, your faith in the promise that God has already approved your request can easily be derailed by performance thinking. Why? It's simple. Your performance is never consistent, and faith only works in a pure conscience. So, when you live under the deception of a "performance gospel," Satan can always make you doubt God's help by convincing you that you didn't _____ enough. (You fill in the blank.)

You must free yourself from this whole "prove yourself" mentality and realize that even your "best performance," isn't really that good. You must believe that God wants to bless you right now, because you're "In Christ," and for no other reason. Read that last line again.

The church has actually withheld a portion of salvation, the financial part, in an effort to get us to behave in a manor that they deem acceptable. Again, this is like being on probation, striving to prove that we will be good citizens of heaven before God will finally trust us enough to grant a **FULL** pardon; one that includes provision. This is totally contrary to the grace of Eph. 2:8 & 9. Sometimes it seems that a major portion of the church doesn't want us to know that we've been **FULLY PARDONED.** It's like they're afraid we might stop trying if we find out we can actually rest in God's salvation.

How does God want us to behave? It's very simple: Love God, and love your neighbor. That's it. End of story.

Now, do you really want to know why so many Christians struggle financially? **Can you handle the truth?**

It is as simple as this: Christians just don't know how to make money.

That may not have registered with you if you've been sitting in church for a long time, but it's true. You've heard time and time again that believers are poor because they're "not giving enough," they're "not serving enough," they're "not as faithful as they should be," they're not "churching" enough, or all of the above.

If you tell me what "camp" your church is a part of, I would be willing to stick my neck out and say that I can probably, in detail, lay out what their criteria for qualifying to receive money from God, consists of. But, the usual church criteria won't contain the real answers for getting you the money you want, and desire. And this is probably true in most any variation you might hear. Their "heaven opening" qualification list will only be the same ole, religious stuff that sounds good to preach, but has never worked for anyone. And we love it because it reminds us of how we've failed God, and that we don't deserve anything good just yet. We're glad to hear, again, that we deserve very little, and we should "just be happy with our poverty" because "someday we'll be ready for more."

Somehow, such preaching soothes us for a time. Maybe this is because it's like receiving our deserved beating for failing God, even though Jesus took one for us. This is the same stuff that's been passed on for generations, mostly by people who are still living hand to mouth, and it only keeps us sedated. I hope that doesn't offend you, but we're trying to deal in the truth here, and that which actually works. Since when is our salvation, and its benefits, based on what we deserve?

Finding a good deal on a "standard Christian issue, used mini-van," after some prosperous sinner is finished with it, is not exactly the pinnacle of prosperity. Due to poor training, many Christians would think they've "finally arrived" with such a deal. If they could only trade up to something with less than a hundred thousand miles on it, they would be close to heaven. And it is good to be content, but I'm trying to point out the low standard we've set due to poverty thinking.

The real problems are very simple and practical. Christians are often uneducated, untrained, unmotivated, unwise, and usually lacking in confidence or self worth. More often than not, they just don't know how to turn one dollar into two, or have anything to offer that others would be willing to pay for. And when they do have something to offer, they don't do what it takes to market their talents. Meager, common efforts will bring meager results; or none at all.

Certainly, giving is a good thing, and it can help or bring a return; but it's not the answer to everything, as many would have us believe. For others to be willing to pay or give us money, we must have something of value in the form of possessions, property, skills, talent, know how, financial worth, or the ability to be an asset to someone else's goals. Financial miracles are very real, and you can get one if you need it, but life will be much easier if you'll learn how to have continuous sources of income.

You can go to church 7 days a week and be the best Christian in town, but if you're not willing to acquire some skills, knowhow, or a marketable degree of some value, get used to the idea of living a very meager lifestyle. Why would anyone want to hire, trade, or do business with you? Who goes to an empty grocery store when they're looking for food?

God can give you money making ideas, but they won't come just because you're a faithful church goer and good rule keeper. They will come because you're seeking ideas, and willing to do what it takes even if it means more education or training. If you'll get this truth in your head without having your feelings hurt, you can do something about your own situation. Sure, we're all precious human beings of value to God, but it takes more than that for someone else on the earth to part with their money in your direction, and that's how the financial world works.

Even when Christians have something to offer, they often don't know how, or they won't try to market their gifting or product. I know people who have great talents in song writing, singing, and performance abilities, but due to laziness, or this idea that God will promote them if He wants to, they never go anywhere. You have to put your hand to something before God will add His blessing. You can write the best song ever, and have the best singing voice in the world, but if no one knows about it, you won't get paid. The odds of being "discovered" without extreme effort and promotion are very slim. And just doing what everyone else has done, usually isn't enough.

Sure, some people get discovered easily, but there are thousands of people who have great abilities and no one has ever heard of them, or will. Time is passing them by because they won't do what it takes. I'm thinking of a man right now who has tremendous talent, but he's waiting on God to "promote" him, and wondering why it hasn't happened yet. His family is struggling financially and in danger of losing their home, but he and his wife won't listen, which is the root of every problem in the world. If I had his singing voice, I'd be marketing myself and singing all over the world, but he just keeps waiting for something to happen, and he's not getting any younger.

I remember when I was a young and dumb minister waiting for the phone to ring. Day after day, I just couldn't believe that no one was calling, especially since I had so many great things to say. The Lord finally got it across to me that "pastors won't call you if they've never heard of you." And even if they have, they're always too busy to take the first step. He clearly said, "You must pursue them!" So I started doing just that. After a while, I had a full schedule.

Pay attention to Solomon as he addresses these two major problems. Number 1, "Listen, and let your words be few"... And Number 2, "**For the dream comes through a multitude of business,**" Eccl. 5:1-3. Another version says, "For the dream comes through much effort." In other words, you must work hard and promote your dream if you want it to come to pass. And, you must learn to listen, not only to God, but those who have something to offer. We don't work to impress God, or earn His blessings, but we work hard to promote and accomplish our dreams.

Don't think that things will be fair, because they never are. I know popular ministers who shouldn't even be ministers, yet because they know how to promote their agenda, they have developed a certain amount of notoriety. Due to their diligent marketing, they have many believing that theirs is a valid and important ministry, even though they really have nothing to offer, other than fluff. In fact, they're actually interfering with legitimate ministers who are trying to bring in the harvest. Due to good marketing, and the unfortunate fact that people are so easily deceived, false religions are also a dime-a-dozen. How much more should those who really have something to offer, be laboring to get their gifting before the people?

Through years of ministry, I have learned that you just can't help people who won't listen, and the ones who have the same on-going problems, are these same people. Have you ever observed a political debate where someone has some really stupid political ideas, but when someone else makes a valid contradictory point that's full of wisdom and truth, they don't even hear it? They immediately start talking over the top of the other person, so they never learn anything. Many Christians do this way too, and they simply never listen. They're thinking of their next statement before the person with the truth even finishes their point. A wise person considers.

As a pastor, there were some people who sat under my teaching for years, and as I observe them now, I don't think I even made a dent. I gave them extremely valuable information on how to live and overcome, and they still go out and get deceived and beat up by the devil time and again. You just can't help people who won't listen.

I offered real, proven, advice to the family above, on how to save their home, yet, they didn't really take it in. They just want to voice their opinion and wallow in the thinking that their situation is unfair. They're wondering when God is going to do something, but they won't listen. I've known them for years, and they love to hear all the "super-spiritual" stuff, but never the real answers. It's amazing how some Christians have "itching ears" for all the "new revelation" fluff-stuff, because it sounds so "cutting edge." But, it's usually the simple common sense stuff that will fix their problems.

Above all; learn to listen and hear God. He knows why you've not been healed, why you've not been delivered from debt, or why you've not gotten that job you wanted. He knows why you haven't been promoted, or why your business idea isn't working. You probably have totally different ideas on these things, other than what God knows. But, He can tell you if you would only hear Him, and He's right.

When Peter needed money for taxes, Jesus didn't give him some "prove-your-self obstacle course" before giving him the answer. And He didn't give him some super-spiritual, nebulous, secret, strategy to open heaven and unblock God's flow of blessings. Jesus simply told him where to find the gold he needed. The only thing Peter had to do was "**listen,**" and then do what Jesus said.

God can, but He doesn't usually, make money fall from heaven. Plenty of money is already circulating here on earth, and it will pass you by if you don't learn how to reach out and take yours. You don't know how many opportunities you may have missed just today.

The Christian financial situation, whether good or bad (and it's often bad), is rarely, and I mean almost never, due to following, or not following, the financial protocol of the modern church. It is always due to knowhow, or the lack thereof. I know that will make some people angry, but it's still true. Yes, go to church and be the best Christian you can be, but make yourself knowledgeable, and learn how to make a profit so you can rise above a life of poverty and debt.

After I learned how to win souls and teach it to others, pastors suddenly wanted to hire me to come and teach their congregations. After that, I started getting offers to join church staffs because I had something to offer. No one was calling me before I learned how to teach evangelism. Why would they? I had nothing to offer. Since then, I've also learned how to play the keyboard and lead worship. Now, if I ever need a church job, I have several skills to offer. There are more than a few want ads on Christian job sites for worship leaders who can play an instrument. Of course most churches don't usually pay much for musicians, but some do. They all should, really. It's quite a commitment.

I recently received a prayer request from a woman for her husband to get a much better paying job. They weren't really interested in trying to improve their skills, or learn how to make money, but just wanted a better pay check. As I listened to her explain that he never had a job that paid well, I asked her about his qualifications, which were virtually non-existent. I told her I would pray, but I also explained that they both should think about getting further training to qualify for better paying jobs. I could tell she was somewhat offended by this, but this had been a long, on going, situation.

What does it take for Christians to realize that being a faithful Christian doesn't automatically generate a pay check? The talent traders in Jesus' parable had to use some proficiency. Anyone can start learning today!

Millions of Christians are peddling as fast as they can and trying to convince God to "release" something, while He's already freely given everything. **THERE'S NOTHING LEFT TO RELEASE!** That's right; it's **ALL** been given, **ALREADY**, so there's nothing left to "**release!**" The ball is totally in your court now, and God has already said "YES!" **You have "already" been fully pardoned and accepted! REALLY!**

To make this true in your own mind, it will probably take some real doing on your part. But try not to lose this freedom to the next "How to Get There" sermon you're certainly bound to hear. Guard these seeds for germination, according to Mark 4. Jesus said that Satan comes "*immediately*" to steal the "Word" once it's been planted, and according to Mark 4, the odds are against reaching a harvest.

Right now, as you're reading this, there are thousands of well intentioned, Sunday morning speakers, who are pouring over their Bibles on a quest to connect two or three verses that will, if executed properly, "finally release the flow God's blessings," so be ready. Some of us treat the Bible like some magic "book of secrets" containing a mysterious formula that, if found, will finally destroy the ominous, evil curse.

Well, the Bible actually **CAN** destroy evil curses, but it's no secret unless you've been taught a faulty gospel that mixes in legalism. Then you're on a never ending quest. The real "formula" is simple FAITH IN JESUS' FINISHED WORK OF REDEMPTION, WHICH GIVES US ACCESS TO GOD AND EVERYTHING HE HAS, and due to nothing we've done ourselves.

This *Prove Yourself Gospel,* that permeates much of the church, is not the gospel at all. In fact, it can actually separate you from the grace of God and cause Jesus to profit you nothing, according to Galatians 5. Most of our church legalism is extremely subtle, and often sounds good to our leaven poisoned minds. We accept it without knowing we've been "slimmed," and many will even fight to defend it.

Those who teach such things don't even realize the poison they're using. In a trial, legalism is a destroyer of confidence and a killer of faith and joy, the main ingredients for a victorious life. It will keep you guessing at a time when you need to know exactly where you stand with God. Strong faith will only grow in an environment of knowing you're okay with God. But, legalism doesn't allow this because you're never sure if you did enough of everything you were supposed to do, and there's no way of knowing.

Whenever anyone says, "God will give you money because of _____," and anything other than the word **grace** goes in the blank, you're probably being taught something that's not true. God blesses us because we belong to Him, and that's it! The other thousand reasons you'll hear, have little or no validity at all. Everything comes to us because of sonship and grace. Yes, "free will" giving will bring a return, but the power behind this blessing also comes from grace.

If you'll really listen, you'll hear that much of what is put forth as "free will giving," is often coerced with subtle threats and warnings if you don't "give." Or, there are promises of rewards for things that are already freely a part of salvation. This type of giving is not actually motivated by "free will," but fear. "Free will," is just that. Most Christians don't even notice the coercion because they're so used to it. They think these subtle, little fear tactics are normal, and even godly.

Showing your performance to God, is like informing a willing lender of your bad debts even though they didn't show up on your credit report, and **after** the lender has **already** said **yes** to your request. How foolish would that be? Yet we do this all the time. We think we've been really good Christians, but in the world of grace, our performance only creates a "bad credit report." Isaiah called "our righteousness" nothing more than "filthy rags."

Why would you want to ruin a perfect, blood bought redemption (a clean credit report) with your humanity and lame efforts to make yourself righteous? Would you try to touch up a Rembrandt to make it better? You can't improve on perfection; you can only diminish it.

Well, we won't really get into that any further right now, other than to say, again, don't forget Jesus' own story of the Prodigal Son. The Prodigal had it in his mind to *regain favor* with his father by "**proving himself**" as a "servant." But, his father (a type of God) would not have anything to do with this attempt, and fully accepted him right on the spot. There's way more in that story than you've been taught.

And don't forget Jesus' own words about the sparrows that neither sow nor reap, but God still feeds them. This is not a verse that you're going to hear very often on telethons, or at offering time, but the truth is, grace is free and it provides everything. Even God's throne is called, "The Throne of Grace." God honors grace, mercy, and faith. He does not honor religion, opinions, or our own works.

CHAPTER 3

WHO IS THIS FOR?

THIS IS NOT REALLY a book on whether or not Christians are supposed to have money, although I am going to include an excerpt from one of my other books to help you with this issue. You will find it toward the end of this book. This is a work on how to obtain the financial promises to which God has already freely said "YES," because provision and wealth *are* included in our redemption package just as the forgiveness of our sins and physical healing are. These blessings come to us at the cost of Jesus' life and blood. They should not be ignored.

Anyone who says "these things are not for today," clearly does not understand our redemption as defined in Isaiah 53, and other places. Matthew chapter 8 explains that "this redemption" is exactly why Jesus healed everyone who came to Him, without exception. That may not be what they teach at the seminary, but Jesus certainly believed it, and He demonstrated the authority of this truth with power for healing and deliverance everywhere He went. He then said that this same power is for everyone who "believes."

So, what do you believe, and who do you believe? Do you believe Jesus, or do you believe Reverend PHD, who can eloquently explain why God doesn't do miracles anymore? There's certainly nothing wrong with having an education, as long as you include God's power in your knowledge! In fact, I highly recommend a good education, but there is something very wrong with anyone implying that part of God's redemption has "passed away." Much of today's church demonstrates the fruit of such unbelief. Everything in God's Kingdom has to do with believing the right things. This is extremely important.

If you're still trying to figure out if Christians are supposed to be blessed, or if having money is better than not having money, you're probably not going to get very far with the things I'm teaching here. If you believe God is using poverty to teach you a lesson, develop your character, make you a better person, or some such thing, you're going to have trouble trying to follow the Holy Spirit.

If you believe that stuff, you'll foolishly think that every mistake you make, or every bad thing that happens along the way, is God's doing. It is very hard to win in this life if you're trying to fight circumstances, Satan, fear, and/or whatever, while half the time you're thinking God is against you, too. Such thinking makes "you" your own worst enemy.

Also, please know that there is a huge difference in suffering for actually serving Christ, and suffering due to a lack of knowledge, Hosea 4:6. Don't get angry with me, but most Christian suffering is simply due to ignorance. Many of us just don't know God very well, His Word, our New Covenant, or have the necessary training and skills for dealing with life in general. Being persecuted or locked up for preaching the gospel, or just being a Christian, is much different from being poor, sick, and/or defeated because you don't understand redemption or how to master money.

Sure, we can be attacked with lack, sickness, or evil circumstances if we're trying to spread the gospel, but we can overcome these things with the authority Jesus gave in Luke 10:19. These things should be temporary afflictions, and they're caused because we have an enemy who hates us. But they should never be something we embrace as "God's will." God's will is for you to have everything Jesus purchased at the cross, just as it is His will for everyone to come to salvation. If He didn't want this for you, He wouldn't have sent Jesus to the cross.

We know that there are many who won't partake of Jesus' salvation, but that doesn't mean that God didn't provide it for everyone. The choice is ours, and the same is true for every part of redemption, including financial provision.

I know a little bit about suffering for Christ and spreading the gospel; again, it is quite different from just being ignorant about our covenant. I've been that, too. Paul suffered many things because he was constantly preaching salvation and grace, not because God was trying to teach him a lesson, or make him a better person. How many of us are actually doing what Paul did with grace, or even a small measure of it?

If you look closely, you'll find that Paul was rarely persecuted for

Making Money With God

just preaching about Jesus. Most of his persecution came when he tried to explain that the Law was no longer necessary, and that Jesus "alone" was enough for salvation without having to do even the smallest part of the Law. This is when the religious crowd gets angry. All of Satan's authority (the power to accuse) lies within the Law, and the "the power of sin is in the Law," according to I Cor. 15:56. This is why we should avoid practicing the Law and all other forms of legalism, like the plague. You can read more about this in my other books.

Since I've been writing books about grace and finances, many of my ministry friends have disappeared from my life. They think I'm a heretic because I actually believe Ephesians 2: 8 & 9, even when it comes to money. They think I'm strange because I actually think that everyone should experience God's healing power, and His abundant provision. I don't make religious excuses when prayer doesn't get answered; I seek God for the real reason, which is usually a matter of limited faith due to a lack of understanding. But, we never want to admit this fact. We always have a number of other reasons; hence, our denial keeps us from making the necessary adjustments for victory.

People really get angry if you tell them they don't have the faith necessary for a miracle, just as the Pharisees did with Jesus. But this problem is not always the fault of the people. If we don't teach the fullness of redemption, they can't possibly have the faith needed for a miracle. Faith simply cannot grow in the soil of a faulty or limited gospel. "Faith comes by hearing," but we must hear the right thing. So, the good news is: If you need more faith, you can plant for a larger harvest. Or, you can keep plugging along while wondering why God doesn't fix everything for you.

The church has accepted a huge lie that has crippled many people concerning faith. The church often misquotes Jesus' statement about the "mustard seed" saying, "if you have faith the *'size'* of a mustard seed, you can move a mountain." But, Jesus never said this at all! He actually said, "If you have faith *'AS'* a mustard seed (not the size of)..." His point was, though it is a small seed, IT WILL GROW into a huge tree and take over the garden (your thinking); and this is what faith must do before it will move mountains.

Why would Jesus always be rebuking people for having "little faith," if a little was enough to get the job done? That doesn't make sense. Jesus spoke of faith in different measures, from "no faith" to "great

39

faith," and He often used the term "little faith" when describing His dissatisfaction with His disciples. So, the amount of faith we have does make a difference, and this IS UP TO US, not God. Which amount of faith was Jesus pleased with? You can read more about faith in my book *How to Have Great Faith*, if you're interested.

You know, If the Apostle Paul came back today under another name, teaching the grace that he taught, I seriously doubt that he would be welcome in most of today's churches, so I don't feel so bad. I'm not even sure if Jesus would be welcome. He would want to heal everyone, immediately, and that would really upset most of our theology, as it certainly did 2,000 years ago.

Satan hates for Christians to find out about real grace and freedom through faith "only," because then he can't keep them contained. He wants you to always be thinking that you haven't quite done enough for God's blessings, yet. He wants you to always be striving for that elusive "next level," and God's total approval, which you're not supposed to have until somewhere in the distance future. If he can just keep you in that mindset, your faith will never grow much, and you'll never get very far in the true things of God. And you'll probably never really feel qualified for doing much of the ministry that God has for you. Confidence and knowing you're "okay" is the key to moving in God. Jesus was never insecure, nervous, or plagued with self image issues. He knew He was right with God.

If you step out and try to win souls, you'll definitely encounter Satan's resistance as well. Satan doesn't really bother Christians who are very busy with the usual non-fruit-producing, churchy stuff. But, he hates it when churches and individual Christians start winning souls. Be prepared for problems if you're going to win souls, but the fruit and blessings are well worth the effort.

I remember a famous minister once saying, "God really wants to bless you (he was speaking to a crowd), but you're just not ready to receive it yet!" And of course, doing his formula was the way to get ready, which included sending him more money than people had been sending. I was very naïve at the time and I let that one, little, very subtle, religious lie keep me in prison for the longest time. I patiently watched others prosper while I tried to get "ready," and they weren't even saved. It took a lot of work to get such constantly reinforced thinking out of my head, but it's been well worth it.

Even when you're free, though, persecution and troubles will still come. But, they're much easier to overcome when you know that God is not the author of such things, and that He is with you, and has approved of you, **BEFORE** the trial, not after. Just from writing this book at God's leading, which will certainly help many people, I've encountered some huge financial problems, and here I am writing about finances. And guess what, the trouble started the very day I started this book.

Is that a coincidence? I don't think so. Such things happen when we try to rescue people from wrong thinking. Satan often attacks the messenger, but this should be expected and overcome. It is simply a given if you're going to join in the war of saving hostages. Did the Nazis just step aside when the allies came to liberate Europe? I'm not going to stop believing that God wants me blessed just because of some demonic setback. Again, this type of resistance is quite different from just not knowing God's will, redemption, or his promises. Know who the enemy is, and learn to discern the true cause of your problems. It is seldom what we think it is.

Now if you're rebelling against God over some issue, or living in sin, then He might, and probably will, leave you in difficult circumstances, even more so than what comes at us in everyday life from just living in a fallen world. But I'm not going to address all those character issues and the dangers of having money, or loving it. I'm going to leave that with your pastor and write as if everyone reading is living right, trying to serve God, and actually believing that God wants them blessed. This is the way I was for many years, along with most of my friends. We were living right and doing all the right things, but going nowhere.

Believe me, **there are just as many character problems with being poor as there are with having wealth, and maybe more**. We must overcome either way.

Look, God doesn't live in a little shack by the railroad tracks, unless He's there for you. He is a mighty God of abundance and power, and He is surrounded by extreme wealth as is clearly described in the Bible. Even when He was traveling through the desert with Moses, He had a pretty expensive tent. And if you're a real Christian, YOU ARE an "heir and joint heir with Christ!"

Think of that! You're an "heir" to God Almighty Himself! Work at getting that into your thinking! Yes, while here on earth, Jesus said he didn't have a place to lay his head (Luke 9:58), but that was because

"HE BECAME POOR SO THAT YOU MIGHT BE RICH," II Cor. 8:9. Don't you understand that He wasn't trying to teach us how to live in poverty and still be happy! He was exchanging His wealth for our poverty, the result of sin. He did this so you could be blessed! (The context of II Cor. 8 is money. Paul was NOT talking about "spiritual riches!")

Don't let any minister make you think that money itself is evil; or that you can't have money and be a good person at the same time. If money is evil, then we shouldn't have any at all. But, many godly men in the Bible had great wealth and still loved God! And God has great wealth, too. Only poverty minded, religious people, or those who politically prefer that Christians be poor, fight the idea of God having wealth and sharing it with His heirs. Does an earthly king give wealth to his children? Then, how much more should we expect from God?

I said all that to say this: Put away the fine-toothed comb that you use to condemn yourself, and start believing that God really does love you, likes you, and wants to bless you. If He's not specifically speaking to you about some real sin, then move ahead and forget about all that other trivial junk that you think God might be bothered about. He's not. He thinks you're okay. It's you, and those who are telling you "you're not there yet," who are wrong. I would accept God's opinion if I were you. He thinks of you as "in Christ," and "as He is (Jesus), so are we (you) in this world," 1st John, 4:17. That is God's opinion; anything else doesn't count.

But, if you're still convinced that money is evil, or that it will make you corrupt; quickly send all of yours to me. I'll cast the devil out of it and spend it on winning souls and blessing the poor. Listen, money only makes you more of what you already are, good or bad. Just be good; it's not that hard.

If you don't enjoy seeking and spending time with God, you already have a problem, money or not. If your desire is to really be hanging out in nightclubs, or to be doing other worldly things; and you don't really want to go to church, but you do anyway because it's your duty, you're already messed up. If you think an abundance of money will cause you to do these "secret things" that you'd really rather be doing anyway, God knows your heart and it doesn't matter if you have the money to do them or not. God desires a "willing heart" towards Him. You're not

Making Money With God

doing Him a favor by just showing up. Get yourself filled with the Holy Spirit and these old desires will change.

As I said, real faith only works in a clear conscience and it is based on knowing that you're righteous, knowing what is available, and knowing what God's will is for you. It takes faith to hear and follow the Holy Spirit, but how can you have faith if you don't know what's included in your redemption package, or believe that you qualify for it?

How can you place an order in a restaurant if you don't even know what's on the menu? You would just be guessing and hoping for something good to eat, but that doesn't work in God's kingdom, and God's restaurant is free. Faith is to know the answer, and not guess at it. But many of us are guessing and hoping. We've never been taught what is included in the fullness of redemption. Forgiveness of sins is usually about as far as we get. Some have even learned to include healing, but very few know that finances are also a part of redemption. If they did understand this, they wouldn't make it so hard to get God's financial blessings.

If you're watching a movie for the second or third time, then you have complete knowledge of the ending, and that's the way faith knowledge works. You KNOW what's going to happen because you've seen it, and when you KNOW God's Word, you can see the ending. You're not worried and nervous during a movie you've seen, because you KNOW the ending. With faith, you KNOW what's on the menu, and you KNOW what's available in the kitchen, just for the asking.

Faith is NOT the weak, wishful, unsure, stuff that most people think of. Faith doesn't wonder if God's going to help; faith knows. Real faith is powerful and it means business. Real faith won't take no for an answer, even when it looks like there is no hope. If you're in the land of wondering and uncertainty, then it's because you don't know where you stand with God, or you don't know what you've been promised in our covenant.

Jesus said, "Nothing is impossible to him who has faith." And also, "Ask anything in my Name and I will do it." God wants to help you and bless you, and your faith can certainly bring the Holy Spirit's leadings to you as well. He doesn't love me anymore than He loves you, but I spend time asking for His leading, fully expecting it to come. He is very generous, so start asking right now. God will answer. It may not be immediate, but He will answer because He's faithful.

A. Bruce Wells

I recently heard some news about a possible shortage of chocolate in the world, due to cocoa farmers abandoning theirs farms in Africa. You can buy cocoa on the commodities market, so I started asking God if I should. For some reason I was assuming that He would definitely tell me to buy it, and I started wondering why He wasn't speaking to me concerning this thing. This caused doubt and other questions to come to mind, so I really started seeking Him. Still, no leading came. Well, as it turned out, God's silence *was* a leading, because in a very short time, the price of cocoa fell tremendously. I had forgotten my own rule, "If God's not saying anything, don't do anything." My point: God is always faithful.

CHAPTER 4
LET'S GET STARTED

IT'S AMAZING HOW WE know that if someone wants to play the piano, he or she must "learn" how. Or if someone wants to do brain surgery, again, they must learn how. But strangely, Christians have this idea that if they can just faithfully be the best Christian they can be, do their Christian duties, whatever they may be, then money will come to them. And they'll live this way for years while waiting for God to finally make something happen.

But in the mean time, non-churched people, who are often without all the Christian hang-ups concerning money, are out making money hand over fist. They do this simply because they've learned how to do it. But, the faithful Christians are still waiting to be accepted by God, or they're waiting for some future "breakthrough" that's going to fix everything.

My point is this: Anyone can learn to make money, with, or without God. But how much better should the Christians be at it, if God is with them? Making money is a learnable skill, like driving a car. Some people are better drivers than others, but anyone can improve with practice. So, start LEARNING how, today! The "breakthrough" you need, is in your head.

There are opportunities all around you every day! If you'll only start praying and looking for the opportunities God will send, and make yourself ready to pounce when they appear, you'll start to prosper. If you can just get in the habit of making a profit with more regularity than spending your money on whatever, you'll never be in lack again. Even now as I'm writing this, I could tell you of 2 or 3 commodities that are soon to move in a certain direction. But, if I was somehow able to

A. Bruce Wells

tell you, and you don't know how to trade, you wouldn't be able to do anything about it even if you knew exactly what was going to happen.

That incident with the BMW didn't just happen by chance. I am always asking God to show me opportunities. In fact, that same day I was riding in my car asking God to show me how to make a profit. I often ask Him to show me how to double a certain amount of cash that I might be using that day, or week. I ASK for these things to happen, and they do. Sometimes I have to wait, but they always come.

It's very true that the rich get richer and the poor get poorer, and there's a good reason for this. It's because the rich have something to work with, and they know how to use it. When a rich person (the prepared) sees an opportunity, he or she is able to act, but when the poor person (the unprepared) sees and opportunity, wishing is the only thing that can be done, or complaining. But, usually, they won't even see the opportunity because they're not trying. They have nothing to work with, so they "think," so why bother looking. If you just give money to the poor without training them, it will soon disappear.

The rich are looking for ways to make their money work for them, but the poor are usually looking for ways to work for money, unless they're the unmotivated, non-working type. If that's the case, the government is their only hope. The government has crippled millions of people by trying to help them. Their help is not unlike that of helping a baby chicken get out of the egg. Such "help" will cause the baby chicken to die because it was deprived of the opportunity to develop the strength needed to survive, just as the welfare state deprives their dependants of imagination, dignity, and motivation.

Jesus also said that the rich will get richer, and the poor will get poorer. Only He said it this way: "He who has will receive more, but he who has not, will lose even that which he thinks he has." If you want to remove yourself from the poor category, you must make yourself ready to take action for something better. If you're not geared up and ready, you'll just sit by and watch others do it while complaining that "life's not fair," or, "there's no *social justice*." And guess what: **Life is not fair, and it never will be! There is NO SUCH THING AS *FAIR*!** Don't even waste your time thinking about such things. Just go out and win!

When I made my first trade/investment, I didn't know how to do much of anything. (In my mind, a "trade" is short term, while an "investment" is long term.) In fact, my first trade was a penny stock (a

Making Money With God

stock under $5 per share), and I had to get someone else to "put the trade on" for me. I didn't even know how to open an account. No one is born knowing these things, but you can read and question those who know. You don't have to be ignorant forever. If you've learned how to walk and talk, you can learn how to make money.

When my oldest son started going to grade school in southern Indiana, he would go to the store and buy candy and gum before school. Then he would sell it to the other kids at school for a profit. They were glad to pay it, too. They had no access to this stuff at school, and what kid doesn't want some candy or gum in the middle of the day at school? Supply and demand created a market place right there in school, and this is essentially the way the whole world of money works. Buy and sell, supply and demand; in a nutshell, that's all there is to it. Learning to multiply this process is the real challenge, and the secret to great wealth.

When discussing trading, I'm amazed at the number of people who say, "Well, I don't know anything about that stuff," as if they've been barred for life from learning anything new. Don't be a lazy, fearful, sheep-minded Christian. Move ahead and take some chances! There are some trading brokers that will let you open an account with no money, but of course you have to fund your account(s) before you can actually trade. At least you're moving the ball forward, though, by just opening an account.

It is almost as simple as opening a bank account, and some brokers will even give you a checkbook or VISA debit card to access your funds. Others will mail you a check, or wire funds, whenever you like. You can put a little money in your account on a regular basis, just like with a savings account. Some even pay interest, and after you build your account up with a few deposits, you can start trading.

I had scraped together an extra $500, a lot of money for me at the time, and I started asking God how I could double it. I decided to not touch this money and just use it for investments only, which is a major key. Deciding to not touch your trading "stake" is an important decision, and often hard to stick to. When you've been living under a spirit of poverty, as I did for many years, something calls for that money everyday. Satan doesn't want you to have anything to work with, and he'll try his best to make you spend your capital, if you let him. He wants you living hand to mouth like all the other Christians, financially crippled and unable to move ahead.

As far as spending your profit goes, you must pretend that your trading money doesn't even exist until it grows enough to start taking a small percentage. Otherwise, you'll always be starting over. After you get your account built up, start risking smaller percentages because you will be occasionally wrong. Always protect your working capital so you can trade again on another day. Limiting your risk, as every seasoned trader will tell you, is the most important of all trading rules. You can't trade again if you lose it all on one trade.

For several days, I just kept bothering God about showing me a trading opportunity. Pretty soon, He started to give me some direction. I had already heard about an energy stock from a friend of mine, and then on the next Sunday morning at church, another friend started telling me about the same stock. It was selling for only pennies per share. Well, my ears perked up some, but then that evening, a third person called me to tell me something and he mentioned the same stock. I thought this was very unusual, so I took it to prayer.

You'll find that God often uses repetitive incidents to get our attention, so if something keeps coming before you, pay attention, but don't try to make this happen. You'll get deceived if you do. Some Christians say that there are no such things as coincidences, or accidents, but this is not true. We must learn to discern if something is really a sign from God, a coincidence, or even something demonically inspired.

Jesus said, in the story of the Good Samaritan, "By *chance*, a priest came along..." Please notice what Jesus didn't say. He didn't say, "God sent, or allowed, or willed, that this priest be there at that very moment." Again, it was by chance. God doesn't order, or design every thing that happens in this world, as many erroneously believe. You have a big say in the events of your life, and there are other forces at work, too. We must "discern" what is God, and what isn't.

As I was praying, I asked the Lord if this was the investment answer to my prayers. Well, with this very humorous feeling, I heard a very clear, "YES, what are you waiting for?" So I called a friend and asked him to place the trade for me, which he did.

Well, within just a matter of days, the $500 became $2,000 and I had no idea why. I was only asking God for a "double," and of course He did better. I just did what God told me to do and I was amazed

Making Money With God

that the Lord was interested in my finances. It was only a matter of buying something (in this case, some shares) that someone else would be willing to pay more for. This happens almost every time anyone, anywhere, buys something. You'll find profits being made this way in every realm of life.

Walmart builds huge, expensive stores and warehouses, just to fill with items that they bought at wholesale prices. Then these items sit and wait for someone to buy them for more money than Walmart paid. It's "candy & gum" all over again. You can do the same thing without having the huge building overhead. Just fill your inventory with wholesale priced stocks, or commodities, and someone else will buy them. You don't have to store them, or even see them. They're just blips on a computer screen that can make you money.

I have bought thousands of bushels of wheat, corn, and soybeans, and I've never even laid eyes on any of them. The beauty of trading futures is that you sell them well before the "delivery date." Every kernel of corn is bought and sold thousands of times before it ends up on your plate. The only "overhead" you need is a computer, a phone, and some working capital. And the only catch is, waiting for God to tell you when the price is right. Believe me, there is always something somewhere that is priced way lower than it should be, or way higher. You can even make money on falling prices as well, which will be discussed later. It's called "shorting" the market, not to be confused with a real estate "short sale."

A real estate "short sale" is the act of selling a house for less than the loan "pay-off," with the bank's agreement, of course. This was unheard of before our government went crazy with the housing market, but now it's quite common. So, does the bank lose money on a short sale? Well, during the negotiations, they'll act like they're losing money, but through the FDIC and special provisions for the banks, the tax payers actually make up the difference, and then some. The banks often come out better on these "short sales" than with regular pay-offs. This is the miracle offspring of Washington and Wall Street sleeping together and scratching each other's backs, at the tax payer's expense.

Let me briefly warn you to be very cautious with "penny stocks." Even though God helped me with that first trade, penny stocks are not usually a good investment and they're ***extremely*** risky, even to the point

A. Bruce Wells

of being foolish. Plus, they're often associated with fraud and a number of scams, such as the common "Pump and Dump" scam.

The "Pump and Dump" people buy huge amounts shares and then advertise (emails, word of mouth, etc.) and really push them just to get them to move a few pennies, say from 20 cents per share to 30. They only want to attract enough new investors to make their stock move enough for them to get out (dump) with a quick profit. This huge exit causes the price to drop and leaves everyone else holding worthless shares. These stocks are always presented as "hot" shares that are about to go to a dollar, or even way higher, but they almost never do. Always listen to God, and be skeptical. Don't listen to the touts.

Christians often fall for such schemes, and many others. Around church, these things are usually put forth as a way "to finance the gospel, for the end time harvest." Or we're told, "This is the way for the *great end time wealth transfer* to take place." In 30 years of ministry, I've seen a number of churches get involved in suspicious money making endeavors, with everything from gold mines and diamonds, to miracle healing juices and every other multilevel plan you can think of.

These thing are always pushed by someone "who has a friend, who knows someone who has a cousin, who has another friend, who's making $10,000 per week while only working 3 hours a month." When presented with great enthusiasm, as they always are, the hype around these marketing ideas works to gain new recruits who will fill their garages with the new "ground breaking" products, again and again. Once in a great while, one of these plans might actually work, but most just fade away after involving much of the congregation in the frenzy. Often, people are left disappointed and wounded because you can only keep them "hyped up," with no real results, for so long.

Church is often the perfect breeding ground for the right con, especially when the members are naïve, trusting of men, and eagerly waiting for that elusive, all at once, "financial breakthrough." You know; that "great money outpouring" that will happen when the heavens finally part and release God's blessings, like a huge, spiritual piñata. Cons love this mentality because, after all, "This could be it!"

The New Testament fails to mention any such event, but it is still presented in many churches as "about to happen," any day now. I guess this gives the church hope since most of what they teach about money hasn't worked, yet. Their blessings are always in the future, which means

Making Money With God

the leaven of legalism is involved. Real faith is always present tense, because it looks at what the cross provided.

"The Great End Time Wealth Transfer," if you want to call it that, happened at the cross, only most Christians don't know it yet. They're still waiting for God to do something more, instead of believing in the fullness of what He has done. How can God give more than His own Son? With Him, He gave us everything He had to give.

Wealth is only a small thing compared to the opportunity of having a living relationship with the creator of the universe. But, He's created plenty for everyone, and He's happy to bring you more than you've ever thought possible. You only need His leading. Quit waiting for the heavens to open, or some "breakthrough" to take place. Start believing in redemption, now!

On the commodities market, right now, you can buy 100 ounces of gold for as little as $4,000 because you only have to put up a small percentage (margin) to buy one contract (100 troy ounces). Then, if the gold moves from $890 per ounce, to $900 the next day, which it could easily do with the reckless government we have right now (2009), you could place a "sell order" and pick up a quick thousand dollars with never even seeing the gold.

Or you could hold the contract, based on God's leading of course, and let the gold go to $1,000 per ounce, which it could easily do in this economy. Then you would have a $10,000 profit from your $4,000 margin (money you had to have in your account to trade). You don't even have to spend the $4,000 to make the $10,000; it only has to be in your account in case you're wrong. Some experts believe that gold will go to $2,000 per ounce because of fear and poor government leadership. They may be right.

Is this type of trade risky, too? Yes, but what isn't? Some risk is legitimate and more easily managed than others. Life itself is risk. You take a risk when you take a shower. There is no such thing as a totally safe investment anymore, not even the government or bank stuff. I've seen people lose great sums of money on so called "safe investments," and again, in my opinion, everything is risky if you're not listening to God. Most people get in their cars to drive across town without any thought of risk, even though the risk is very real. Why? Because they have a desire to get somewhere and they've "learned" how to drive. They

A. Bruce Wells

limit their risk by handling the car with safety. Trading can be handled the same way.

And let me say this, also: If you want to "get somewhere" financially, doing nothing is one of the most risky things you can do! Your money will disappear and this world will pass you by if you're standing still. Sure, you'll make some mistakes and probably lose a few dollars, but if you don't quit, you'll finally get somewhere with more money than when you started. The more you accumulate, the less you need to risk. Again, you want to get to the place where you only risk a small percentage on each trade, and you'll never have to work for money, or be dependant on anyone, or anything, again.

Years ago, a certain university did a study involving hundreds of people who were over the age of 95. In this study, they asked each person what changes they would make if they had it all to do over again. The number one answer that came back was: **"I would take more risks."** And there were many comments about things they wish they had done, but instead, succumbed to fear.

Think of all the people who thought to invest in the infant stages of Google, Microsoft, and Yahoo, but they didn't because they were afraid. Or, they didn't know how. I have some of those stories myself. Think of those who had an idea for a product, but then did nothing and someone else invented it. Or, those who had an idea for a book, but hesitated until someone else wrote it. Think of those who wanted to date the person of their dreams, but were afraid to ask, and someone else with courage, less qualified of course, won their hand in marriage. We should be cautious, but we should also live life to the fullest, and that means taking calculated risks. We don't want to be foolhardy, but don't forget the guy who buried his talent of gold due to fear.

Why did Jesus call that guy "lazy?" Because he didn't take the time and effort to learn or investigate what it would take to make a profit. This lack of knowledge is what made him fearful. Let me say that again; a lack of knowledge will produce fear, but information and knowledge will bring confidence. I would be afraid to fly an F-18, but the guy who has learned how and has experience, is just as confident as I am when I drive my car. Having knowledge removes the "unknown," which causes the fear.

We all make mistakes, and sometimes we can have dull hearing. But, with stocks and commodities, you can always place a "stop loss order" under your purchase. With our example above, let's say you place a stop loss order at $885 per ounce per ounce of gold, just for protection. If you're wrong and the gold moves against you, instead of going up, most of your capital will be saved. Then you simply regroup, lick your wounds, pray more, and go at it again. In such a scenario, you would have lost about $500 of your original $4,000. But, "nothing ventured, nothing gained." This is a small amount of money if you're dealing in markets that could possibly "run" for a while, in your direction. Then you just keep moving your stop loss to protect your profits.

With commodities, it is very easy to be right about the overall direction of a commodity, but still get in on the wrong day. This can be costly, especially if you don't have the stomach to wait for it to turn in your direction. This is why it is imperative that you listen to God without hesitation. If it's a long term trend, you should always enter on a "pull back." Chasing a move can be very costly if you're slow to get in after you have a leading. If you're not sure about the trend, I suggest that you just wait for the next bus, instead of running after the one that just went by, as said before. Otherwise, you might only to get on when it's just about to turn around and go back where you first missed it. I've learned this the hard way. What goes up, in commodities, usually comes back down.

You just have to limit your losses when you're wrong, and let the winners run when you're right. If you do this, you'll come out way ahead. When people don't use safety nets, they get hurt; and this is true in any business you might participate in. God is never wrong, but we don't always hear correctly and there are always several ways to "hedge your bets," which you'll learn as you go.

Can you get started for less than $4,000? Yes, there are many trades you can make for less money. There are mini-contracts available for some commodities, such as gold, and a number of the full size commodity contracts can be purchased for just hundreds of dollars. And stocks come in all shapes and sizes, from penny stocks that literally sell for pennies, to stocks that sell for a thousand dollars per share.

Commodities all have different margin requirements (the amount needed in your account to enter a trade) and your broker can tell you what they are for each product. Right now, you can buy 5,000 bushels of corn for only $1,300 and make $50 for every penny it moves upward. Or you could short the market (speculate that it's going down

A. Bruce Wells

in price) and make $50 for every penny that it moves down, if God leads you to go short (down), instead of long (up). Don't forget; He knows everything.

You can buy crude oil contracts, as well as gasoline, butter, lumber, copper, euro-dollars, rice, and many other items. You can even buy shrimp. Not too long ago, God told me to short (position for a drop) the barley market, so I did and I made a good profit. I wish I had been way more aggressive with that trade because it went down for quite some time, but I started listening to my broker.

With the exception of learning how to function and place orders, it is almost always a mistake to listen to your broker, or anyone else, especially when God is leading you. Brokers always remind me of listening to a non-believing doctor when you're trying to get a healing miracle. My broker is a very nice guy, but I don't like for him to talk to me unless I ask a question. I've had a number of different brokers over the years, and can't remember their advice ever making me any money.

I'll say it again; God knows everything. He knows the short term future, and He knows the long term future. If He tells you about a trade, or a purchase of some kind, don't ask anyone else about it. Just do it. Believe me, I have missed out on a pile of money by listening to others after God had given me a leading. Sometimes, His leadings will not be in line with conventional thinking, or else everyone would be doing it. He'll show you the secret things that are about to happen before everyone else knows about it, if you'll spend time with Him. Then you can really make some money.

I'll probably catch a lot of flack for sharing so much about trading commodities, especially from tradition "investment advisors," but I'm really not suggesting that you try something that doesn't bear witness with you. And you don't have to do what I do to make money. I'm just writing about the things that I happen to know about, with the hope that it will inspire you to seek God for yourself. He will lead you into something that is suitable for you, which may be 180 degrees from stocks and commodities. Many people just don't have the nervous system that's compatible with commodities.

Just to be real here, I want to mention that most of what I'm sharing in this book are my successes. But, don't think for a moment that I haven't had my share of failures. In fact, I've had more failures

54

in money matters than the average person, but I've probably tried more things. I've had times when I felt like a complete failure as a person, and as an investor. But, it is incredibly important to avoid letting what has happened to you on the outside, become a permanent part of "who you are" on the inside.

You are an overcoming heir of God Almighty, so never allow mistakes, setbacks, or criticism change the "I am made in God's image" truth that should be established in your own mind. If this thinking is not established in your mind, you need to go to work. Really knowing that you're accepted by God, and made in His image, is a great feeling if you can maintain the right thoughts. Feelings always come from thoughts, which you can control.

Many of the failures I've experienced have been due to demonic harassment, due to my calling as a minister. But, much of it has also been from my own ignorance, or poor choices. But, after licking my wounds, I've always tried to profit from my mistakes by learning and remembering what I did wrong. A number of my failures have been valuable lessons that have led to wisdom and success. Remember, life's a journey, and much of the fun happens on the trip.

Don't be so naïve as to think that Satan won't try to resist you in your trading, or in other money making ventures. I have encountered a number of strange, demonic happenings that have kept me out of trades, or thwarted my success in some way. But, I never start thinking that it's God who is beating me down when something goes wrong. That is possibly the most damning, wrong thinking in the church today, and it causes Christians to lie down and "take it," without a fight.

Satan will try to sound like the Holy Spirit, cause problems, mislead, distract, and make you want to quit. He'll try many such things to block your increase, but he can't stop you if you persist. Once, I was about to place a trade on my computer when the electricity in my house went out for no reason, right when I was about to execute the order. This killed my internet connection and stopped the trade. It was a perfectly nice day and no one else's electricity in the whole neighborhood had gone out. I should have had a phone card in my computer, but I didn't.

By the time the power had come back on, I had missed possibly the best trade of the year. Had I known how good it was going to be, I would have run to the library to place the order on line, or used my cell phone to place a broker assisted order, but I didn't. I never dreamed

A. Bruce Wells

the trade would move so far, and so fast, so I decided to just wait. This was a huge mistake and I missed out on enough to probably live for a whole year or two.

Was this "black out" just a coincidence? Well, even the repair guys thought it was very weird, and you could just feel that it had that dark, demonic flavor. I'm relatively sure it was a satanic attack. But again, Satan can't keep you down unless you let him. God will show you how to win over his interference, and even get revenge.

So, one of the first practical things you could do to change your life is to open a trading account, or two, if God leads that way. And then, start doing everything you can to get some trading money together. I recommend at least a thousand dollars, but if you can do more, that would be even better. Many commodities brokers won't let you start without at least five thousand dollars, but some will, so you may have to shop around. The same is true with stock brokers, but some of the online companies will let you start with less. For stocks, be sure you get a "margin account," because this will allow you to buy more shares than you actually have money for, if you have a certain amount in your account.

Depending on the amount you have, and the company you use, you can buy 2, 3, or even 4 times the amount of stock you could buy if you only had a non-margin account. If you have a margin account, the broker will actually multiply your buying power for a small percentage, and they'll use the stocks as collateral. If the stocks you buy decrease in value, you may get a "margin call" from the broker, which requires you to place more money in your account, or you could simply sell some of the stocks to get your account back into the safety zone. But, if you're right about the stocks you bought, and they go up, the multiplication factor will increase your profits because you own more stocks than you could have otherwise bought. This is called "leverage," because you can move more, with less.

But again, maybe you don't want to trade stocks or commodities. That's okay. After you get some usable capital together, start asking God how you can double it, or increase it some way. Don't worry that you don't know what to do, because He knows a thousand things that will work. Just keep bothering Him until He shows you how you can double your thousand dollars. Then you'll have two thousand to trade.

Sometimes, God tells me to give some of my trading money to the

Making Money With God

poor, or to a ministry. I consider this a very real investment as well; and when He's leading you, there's always a good return, literally. Several months back, the Lord led me to get someone caught up on their mortgage. Within two hours of mailing the check, another person phoned me and said, "God just told me to give you some money," which just happened to be exactly double, to the penny, what I just put in the mail. No coincidence this time.

I know we're not supposed to talk about our giving, but I'm sharing this for your inspiration and faith. Shortly after the above incident, God led me to make another mortgage payment for someone, which was under a thousand dollars. And again, but within a couple of weeks this time, I was given something worth about 10 to 12 thousand dollars, and I knew in my spirit that this was the harvest for that mortgage payment. You can really have some fun doing this stuff, but not if you're living hand to mouth like many Christians do. Who would you rather be; the one needing help, or the one offering the help? Even Jesus said it is more blessed to give than to receive; and it definitely IS.

I've heard a number of ministers say that their ministries are "fertile ground" for sowing your financial gifts. And while that may be true, in reality, the ***most*** fertile ground anyone can sow in, is where the Holy Spirit directs at any given time. He always knows exactly where the money "should" go, and He'll reward you greatly for working with Him.

There are several TV shows that spotlight people trading various items from attics and pawn shops. You should check them out. They're very interesting and they might give you some inspiration, especially when you see some of the profits they make. But, more importantly than the profit, pay close attention to the negotiating skills used, or lack thereof. You can learn from watching these guys. Ninety per cent of those who are selling just lie down and take the first or second offer, when they could have gained way more if they knew how to negotiate.

One of the easiest ways to trade stocks, and few people take advantage of this, is not through the stock market at all. Instead of picking individual stocks, which takes time and study, or mutual funds (groups of stocks and investors), you can actually trade whole stock market "indexes," such as the DOW, or the S & P. You can do this by placing an order for a contract(s) on the commodities exchange for which ever index you prefer. You are simply betting that the whole market will either go up or down, which is pretty easy to guess if you pay attention to the foolishness in Washington. You can hold your contract(s) for a few minutes, a day, or months, depending on what you believe it's going to do.

A number of people made millions betting that the DOW would fall after the last presidential election (2008), which it did, to the tune of over 4,000 points. The majority of the fall started on "Inauguration Day" because the "smart money" people knew that such a socialist thinker would be a financial disaster, and so far, they've been correct. Those who "shorted the market" (bet that it would go down), cleaned up while everyone else was crying because they didn't get out. They were locked into the thinking that someone else should make your financial decisions, and that you can only make money if the market is going up.

Most investors didn't know, or even consider, that they could control their own destinies by not following the crowd, or that they could bet on the market to go down, as well as up. What ever you decide on for yourself, don't be "sheep-minded," and don't trust anyone else to make your decisions. Nobody will watch your money like you will! Just ask anyone who followed Madoff.

For something on a smaller scale, I know of a woman who buys cheap, little figurines at dollar stores, or anywhere she can find them. She then sells them on eBay for 5 to 10 times what she paid. I know another family that mixes inexpensive, imitation perfumes in their garage, and they make a fortune selling them on the internet. They send out orders all over the world. People will buy almost anything, if you package it right and advertise.

God told me to write books, and I get an ever increasing royalty check every quarter. Thank you for buying this one. Plus, there are several other things I can do for money. I recommend everyone should have multiple sources of income. That way, you're not devastated if something dries up, or you lose your job. Just as traditional "buy and hold" investing is not as safe as it used to be, the idea of having only one skill, or one career, is also very risky in the world we now live in.

Maybe back in a time of more honor and honesty, our grandfathers could afford to be loyal to one company and career. But today, who

Making Money With God

knows if your pension will even be there when you need it, or that you won't be laid off one year before retirement. Company loyalty to devoted employee is almost a thing of the past. Survival and profit are the major forces at work now, especially with our own government taking more and more of the lion's share and regulating the very life out of most every business.

I know very well what it's like to suffer lack and tremendous financial problems, and there's no way I would ever again allow myself to not have several streams of income. I've had businesses fail; I've been evicted; I've dealt with collectors; and I know what it's like to have the bottom fall out of all my plans. I know how it feels to be rejected, unemployed, embarrassed, shamed, and humiliated. I've even prayed that I could just lie down and die, but God had other plans for me, as He does for you. So, pull yourself up and start learning some new tricks.

Now, I'll always have an alternate source of income. I'll never, ever, put my financial well being at the mercy of other people, as I did as a minister for so many years. I hold a contractor's license, a real estate license, I'm an ordained minister, I have management experience, I do church growth consulting, ministry speaking, counseling, and I'm a writer. I even get paid to play music sometimes. I trade stocks, commodities, cars, boats, property, and just about anything else I can make a profit on; and if I had any more time, there are several invention ideas I would like to pursue.

If one of these sources dries up, it won't be a disaster like I've experienced in the past, and I'm not waiting for a "breakthrough," as is just about every Christian I know. What can you add to your provision? God has many ideas that you've yet to consider.

I never thought to be an author, but God thought I should. I'm not someone who enjoys sitting at a computer for long stretches of time. Writing was totally His idea. If you haven't realized this by now, you should consider that God is possibly way smarter than we are, so we should listen. There's no telling what you're capable of that you've never even thought of.

I heard a young man once say, "The job I'm doing now is the only thing I'm good at," and he said it like he would never be good at anything else. I replied, "How do you know what you're really good at, you've never even tried anything else." Now, he has a much better job, and there are still many other things he could master.

59

Ask God for ideas. Read everything you can get your hands on. If you don't have a product or service to sell for a profit, you'll simply have to go and get something. If you can just put your hands on something that others might want, you'll make a profit. Look for a piece of real estate to flip. Start a small business. Find something to sell, even if you have to make it.

Who would have believed that Pet Rocks would sell, but some guy got rich selling thousands of them. Just buy something at a low price and then resell it, like I do with stocks and commodities. Package that great tasting recipe of yours, and market it. Chef Boyardee was unheard of until he did exactly that; and in my opinion, most of his stuff doesn't even taste very good. I know someone who makes the best looking Christmas wreaths you'll ever see, but I've never been able to talk her into selling them for a profit. She always has some reason why it won't work. Do you know anyone like that?

Whatever you obtain to sell, make sure it is something that many people would want. Don't try to market something that only a very few would be interested in, like hot air balloons, or a deep sea diving bells. "Bread and butter" items are always best, like a 4 door sedan, or a 3 bedroom, 2 bath house. Such a home will be in much more demand than a 2 bedroom, 1 bath, or a house that has a railroad track going to through the back yard. A 4 door, automatic sedan is way easier to sell than a 2 door with a standard shift, and white pickup trucks are gravy. I'm very careful to only trade commodity markets that are liquid (a high volume of traders involved). Otherwise, you might not be able to get out instantly, if necessary.

During a "recession," you can make extremely low offers on boats and other such things. Even many of the traditional big name stocks might sell for just a few dollars during a recession, when they normally sell for $30, $40, & $50 per share. Unless it's the end of the world, such stocks will probably go up again some day. When people are fearful, they'll often sell things for only pennies on the dollar. I saw a mobile home the other day that was selling for only $1,500. It wasn't fabulous, but it was livable, and someone would love to own it for $5,000.

You could go door to door collecting junk. Everyone is storing junk they would love to get rid of, and somebody else will be glad to buy it from you. Used furniture is big business in South Florida. Do you know someone who's making money? Do what they're doing, only do

Making Money With God

it better. Mr. Post copied everything that Mr. Kellogg was doing, and made millions.

If someone is asking $10,000 for their boat, offer them $4,000. The worst that can happen is they'll say "no." If they do say "no," leave your name and number. Never be in the position where you "have to have" something. After their offended pride settles, they may call you with a counter offer. If you get it for $6,000, you can sell it for $8,500. These are the kind of things you can do if you're not desperate like everyone else. And if you have good credit, you don't even have to lay out any cash. I've done this type of thing many times with my own money, and with borrowed money.

I saw a "like new" SUV one day that had a for sale sign asking $14,500, and it was worth every penny. So I called the guy, test drove the vehicle, and offered him $11,000. (Showing a lot of interest during the test drive will make a seller hungry for "the sale.") After he said "no way" to my offer, which I expected, I gave him my number and went home. The next day, I bought it for $11,250, which was well below the book value. I was going to resale it, but I liked it so much, I kept it. It was great for pulling a trailer.

"Oh, but isn't that taking advantage of people?" No, not if they agree to it. I didn't twist his arm, and he called me back. Most everything in life is a matter of negotiation. When you pass up something you want at the grocery store, it's probably because you're looking for a better price. You're saying "no" to their price by not buying, and if enough people do that, the price will come down.

When someone is selling something, everyone wins if they make a sale, and you get a deal that you can profit from later. This is the way the whole world operates. But, again, if something bothers your conscience, don't do it. If you feel you should help a particular person, then go with your leading. You can pay full price, or more, if you like. But, also consider that it might be an opportunity for God to bless you. Don't forget, according to the Bible, "The wealth of the wicked is laid up for the righteous."

"But Bruce, I don't have a thousand dollars, and I don't know how to get it!" You can get it if you try hard enough! You probably have more than a thousand dollars worth of junk in your garage, or you could take a part time job. If someone offered you a beautiful new house for only a thousand dollars, you would find a way to get it. If you're going

A. Bruce Wells

to think up a bunch of reasons why you can't do this, you're not going to go far at all.

You need to become a "can do person!" Quit making excuses and reasons for not trying, or for putting things off until tomorrow. Remove the word "can't" from your vocabulary; GOD IS WITH YOU! The thousand dollars you come up with today, could turn into millions if you'll listen to God. You would only have to double your money ten times and you're a millionaire. And, the more money you have, the more plentiful the opportunities. It's true that "the rich (those with trading money) get richer, and the poor (those without trading money or initiative) get poorer." If you don't want to have a lot of money, then give it away to those who are trying to save souls, or to the poor.

A contactor friend just recently did some work for an elderly woman in our city, and he told me she would get up early every morning, turn on several computer screens at her desk, and check her stock and commodity positions. Then she would pray, "Okay Lord, what should we buy, and what should we sell, today?" And God would lead her to do the right thing; in fact, over 4 million dollars worth of right things since she started just a few years ago. Notice that she didn't just buy some shares and hold them for 30 years without thinking. She, with God's help, was actively managing her accounts for the best returns.

This same contractor also told me of another friend who, recently, was told by God to buy silver. Then, during the following month, silver rose over a couple of dollars per ounce. Just one contract (5,000 ounces) of Comex silver (New York silver), gains $50 for every penny it moves. So, a $2 rise on 5,000 ounces would give the contract holder a profit of $10,000, and you only have to have $4,000 in your account to buy one contract. And as long as you're going to sell the contract before the "delivery date," which is normally months away, you don't have to pay the remaining balance. One silver contract is worth about $125,000 ($25 per ounce) in today's market, but you can control, and keep, all of the profit for only $4,000.

This is kind of like buying a house for $4,000 down and then selling it a month later for a $10,000 profit, before having to pay the mortgage balance. If you liquidate before the balance comes due, you're controlling a large amount of money with very little down. Again, this is called leverage (moving much with little). Speculators do this type of stuff everyday.

Making Money With God

What did the two above people have that you don't? Nothing, other than maybe a little capital, the know how to place orders with their brokers, and the courage to risk something. That's all it takes to rise above the rat race of being controlled by money, or the lack thereof. Are you a slave, or a king? Everyone is one or the other.

Wouldn't you love to be going to your favorite breakfast place in the morning to surf your computer, read a book, or to just sip some coffee before going to spend the day doing what you've decided to do, and NOT someone else? Other than our loved ones, time is our most valuable possession, and it's a shame to give so much of it to other people's dreams (creditors and employers) when we could be living our dream. There's nothing wrong with working for someone else, if that's what you want; but you only have so many days on this planet.

How would you like to have bought ten thousand shares of Google when it first went public? Start putting your trading capital aside today because God might show **YOU** the next Google, or Facebook! You don't have to be the one who invents the next Google. You don't even have to know how it works; you just have to be one who knows about it.

Guess who already knows which companies, and/or items, will soar. Maybe He'll tell you. Will you be ready?

CHAPTER 5

LEARNING TO HEAR GOD?

Wow, WHAT A QUESTION. And what an amazing gift from God, that He would actually communicate with us if we so desire. But, how does this take place?

You're going to hear a thousand different opinions on this subject, from "it's not possible to hear God," to "anyone who thinks they're hearing from God is crazy." So, what should we believe? There is a very large segment of the church that doesn't believe that God talks to people anymore, or does much of anything else for that matter. They think that God pretty much did everything He was going to do with the remaining original apostles. And if you didn't get a "word" from God through the last breath of the last living apostle, then that's just too bad because God's not saying anymore. Does that sound as ridiculous to you, as it does to me?

Then at the other end of the spectrum, you have those who think that every thought they have is from God, and if the traffic light turns green while they're praying, it's a sign from God. We've all met such people, and they do very well at making all Christians look nutty. I even know people who have married totally incompatible, and sometimes crazy, partners because they were "led" by such signs. You'll see what you want to see if you already have your mind made up, especially if you're hormones have taken over.

But, is there a way to find the real voice of God, and can we learn to separate His voice from the many others that would cloud our thinking, or pretend to be Him? And how can we possibly be spiritual enough to hear God, without going to some mountain top?

Let me address this common quest of trying to "be spiritual" enough. First of all, you **ARE** a spirit, and you live in a body. Quit trying to "be

Making Money With God

spiritual," and realize that everything about you is spiritual. It is your very essence, as is it everyone else's. When your body dies, the real you, which exists now as a spirit, will only change addresses. Every person (spirit) will exist forever; it's just a question of "where," depending on what each of us does, or doesn't do, with Jesus.

You're a spirit, God is a spirit, demons are spirits, and angels are spirits. So, it's not really that big of a deal to be "spiritual." It's what you ARE. Many people are afraid of demon spirits simply because they are what they are, *spirits*. But, you talk to a spirit (human) every time you talk to another person. There's absolutely no reason to be afraid of demons, unless you're cooperating with them. In fact, they're actually afraid of you, if you know who you are "in Christ." But, they know if you know this, or not. And if you don't, they will surely take advantage.

Probably, the scariest part of encountering a demon, or demons, because they're seldom alone, is being face to face with the stark reality that the spiritual realm of angels and demons really does exist. And that reality means that judgment and a literal hell really exists, too. Suddenly, they're not just Bible stories anymore, and the breathtaking, solemn awareness of eternity and judgment starts to settle in. Everything takes on a different face with the alert consciousness of the invisible. If you ever start winning souls regularly, you will certainly discover the world of demons; but you'll also find that God is with you every step of the way.

When you start talking to people about Jesus, you'll be amazed at how the phone will start ringing, car horns will blow, or a baby will start crying. Interruptions will come from everywhere if you haven't used your authority to spiritually stop such things in advance. When someone from church asks you to come with them to talk to a family member about being saved, and if you don't pray first, other relatives who haven't called or visited in 10 years, will show up at the same time with unruly toddlers and a barking dog. The world of darkness is very real, but so is the world of God and His angels.

Sometimes, demons will manifest when you're winning souls. I've encountered such manifestations a number of times in 30 years of ministry. They're much more common than most people realize. Countless human beings, including many Christians, are influenced by demons to some degree. They are the cause of many of the problems that people request prayer for. This is especially true in the sickness and disease department. I don't believe there is "a demon behind every tree," but I certainly believe in taking a look behind the tree.

This is another reason it is very important to learn to hear God. He knows what you're dealing with when you can't see it. In counseling sessions, no one will ever tell you the whole story, and the cause of their problem(s) is seldom what "they" think it is. But, God knows the real cause, the real answer, and something that is often over looked; the real question. And guess what, He will reveal it if you're tuned in.

One of the reasons so many prayers fail in the areas of sickness and disease, is because no one deals with the demon(s) behind the scenes. Jesus didn't pray for people the way most Christians do. God commanded **us** to "cast demons out," but we want **Him** to "take this sickness away." And if you are trying to cast out devils, but you haven't learned to hear the Holy Spirit, how will you know when the demon is really gone? They will "submarine" and act like they're gone when someone is using authority, hoping that the minister will give up. So, you can't go by what you see.

Again, we ask God, "Please take this sickness away, if it be thy will," which is the most unscriptural prayer in the world. Then we make excuses when this doesn't work, and we develop whole, erroneous theories on why God doesn't want to do for us, what He always did for Jesus. Jesus commanded his apostles to heal the sick, but you would be hard pressed to find that kind of faith today. You can't give what you don't have, and our churches rarely teach the faith that is sufficient for miracles. We're too worried about scaring people away, plus, we're only going to ask God to do what He told us to do, "if it happens to be His will on that day."

What would you think of a policeman who keeps calling the mayor on his cell phone to beg him to come and stop the traffic, or write a ticket, because the cop doesn't know how? That's the average Christian of today, and we're supposed to all be ministers representing heaven, with the ability to connect people with God. That's exactly what the word "priest" means, but it takes real faith and knowhow to bring God's power on the scene.

Some people are totally controlled by devils, like the Gadarene Demoniac in the Bible. While others are only slightly controlled, like someone who can't stop thinking evil thoughts, or overcome an addiction. The religious leaders who hate Jews are certainly demonized, as is the seductive woman who's out to ruin a marriage. You can also include the politician who's drawn to darkness, and every action he or she takes is against righteousness. It's amazing how without even hearing what they plan to do, you know how such a person is going to vote on any moral issue.

Even the Christian who can't stop looking at porn is no doubt partially demonized; and the one who is just toying around with it, certainly will be sooner or later. Sin is an open door for demonic activity. Many don't know this, but demon controlled people are often as normal looking as the next guy, just like the man who had the unclean spirit in Mark chapter 1. We think they will have fangs and their eyes will be glowing red, like in the movies; but the man in Mark 1 probably looked totally normal, and no one knew he had a demon until Jesus showed up.

Apparently, the usual ministers didn't have enough authority or power to stir the thing up. The Bible says this man had an "unclean spirit," or a "sexually lewd" spirit, as indicated in the original text. Possibly, it was a homosexual demon, or some other type of sexual perversion. There's a spiritual reason that some men are attracted to other men instead of women, and the psychiatrists know nothing about this. The same is true for women. Homosexuality is definitely a demonic problem, and it can be fixed.

These things are not just "alternative lifestyles;" they are rebellious and lewd deviations from the way life is meant to be; plus, they amount to cooperation with the demonic realm. Such lifestyles provide "homes" for demons as their influence is spread by association, suggestion, and acceptance. We should love and reach out to these people, but not accept their life style as normal. This only encourages others to experiment and fall into the same life of hell. Gay people are not really "gay" (happy) people, like TV would have you believe. They're usually miserable. Some are relentless in their attempt to finally make this perversion socially vogue, but this is only their attempt to find peace. Repentance with deliverance is the only true answer.

When was the last time you saw a movie that didn't feature "token" homosexuals, suggesting that their perversion is normal? Even our legislators are helping to spread this societal breakdown. What will be next; the right to marry animals, or children? It's happened before

A. Bruce Wells

in history. They're trying everything they can to make homosexual perversion acceptable, but nothing can legitimize this deviant lifestyle, not even same-sex, marriage.

Demons occasionally speak up when confronted, but usually they just lay low while projecting their evil thoughts into their host victim's mind. A young man heard me speak on this subject in California and then requested prayer. He decided he wanted to be free from homosexuality, which is vital for overcoming this sin. Without touching him, I prayed for his deliverance and commanded the evil spirit to come out. Instantly, he doubled over as if someone had punched him in the stomach and then he started to gag as the demon came out.

The unclean spirit, which he picked up by entertaining wrong thoughts and experimentation with another young man, came out because we gave it no other choice. The young man went home rejoicing, totally free from an evil desire that really came from the unclean spirit. If the desire returns, and the young man strongly says "no," he'll stay free and it will get easier and easier. But if he yields to the temptation, prompted by the demon, things will only get worse than they were before.

Sometimes demons will actually speak through individuals. This usually happens when someone is praying for someone, or trying to minister in some way. They do this when they're afraid of being cast out. They'll even scream or do other bazaar things, just like in the Bible. We have no idea how many thoughts humans have that come from the world of darkness, from suicide and depression, to greed, murder, lust, addiction, false religion, wicked politics, and a thousand others.

I was once in a parking lot trying to persuade a young man to ask Jesus into his life, but he wasn't interested. His attitude was, "Yea, yea, I've heard it all before." So I stepped back and asked God to give me something to help the situation. Then, in that "still small voice," God whispered his name, "Charles." So, I asked, "Is your name Charles," and he responded, "How could you possibly know that?" When I told him that God had just spoken his name to me, his attitude changed immediately and he listened to everything I had to say, with great attention. But, that's not the end of the story.

Several days later, I was passing out tracts on a busy downtown street, a well dressed business man came walking up to me, got right in my face, and asked, "Can you tell me what my name is?" Then he quickly

Making Money With God

ran off down the street. It was very strange, but it demonstrates the reality of the realm of demons. This man (actually, the demon spirit in him), knew about the incident in the parking lot with Charles. Demons can network and pass information. This is why some are called "familiar spirits" in the Bible. They're familiar with certain people, circumstances, and/or events. This is how some psychics can fool people. They're tuned in to the demon world, but they think it's "all" God.

Do you remember in the book of Acts, when the demons said, "We know who Paul is, but who are you?" Just make sure you're not in the "who are you" crowd, by learning your authority, and using it. Cast one or two demons out of their comfortable home(s), and they'll soon know who you are, too.

Anyone who knows their authority over demons should be a nuisance to the demonic community. This should be every Christian, but again, such authority (Luke 10:19) is seldom taught in church, and the demons normally just lay low when any ministry is taking place. Plus, most Christians are commonly taught that any of the bad stuff in their life, whatever it may be, is "God's will" because He "allowed" it. Consequently, they really never learn to fight, or possess the land. They just learn to "lay there and take it." In reality, "we" are the ones who allow this "bad stuff," not God. Jesus gave us authority so we could "disallow" this stuff, according to Luke 10:19.

True repentance is often enough to send most demons packing, but there are some that must be expelled by someone with authority. The Bible is very clear that some demons are more wicked, and stronger, than others. It might interest you to know that casting out devils was **one third** of Jesus' ministry. So, just maybe, we should give it a little more attention.

(**Caution to ministers**: If you get involved in the ministry of casting out demons, it is a good idea to have "hold harmless" release forms signed by everyone involved for legal protection. Strange things can happen when dealing with this type of ministry, and I've seen law suits brought against some ministers. Litigation seems to be the new national pass time.)

"Brother Bruce, I just don't believe there are demons in our nice, dignified, church!" If there are people in your church, you can be sure demons are there, too. You may not want to know about this reality, or deal with it, but it is an absolute fact. If God ever opens your eyes to the spiritual realm while you're sitting in church, you will be shocked. The church's "attendance numbers" are much greater than you know, and Satan is an expert at religion.

Getting back to hearing God though, again, what should we believe? A good place to start would be to look at the Bible and the way God spoke, led, cautioned, impressed, revealed, and made known His thoughts and desires. We wouldn't even have a Bible, or know about God, if He wasn't willing and able to communicate with us. And even though many would try to caution you about God talking to you; God says, "Come and let us reason together." Isa. 1:18

Some Christians believe that because God gave us the Bible, He stopped talking to mankind because "we now have The Book." And that seems to be good enough for them. But, what "normal" human father would be so uncaring as to just leave some written instructions without wanting to spend time with his children, and actively speak helpful things into their lives?

Jesus died and gave us the Holy Spirit specifically so God could enter into a personal relationship with everyone. We should read the Bible as much as possible, but learn to listen to the voice of the Holy Spirit as well. God doesn't want to have to find just ONE man to speak for Him, like Moses did. He wants to talk to all of His children. HE WANTS TO SPEAK TO YOU, PERSONALLY!

There are many specifics about your life that are not covered in the Bible, and God is very willing to tell you what to do. The Bible doesn't tell you who to marry, where to live, where to work, where to go to church, or many such things. But, it is God's pleasure to show you His love through many forms of communication. Sometimes God will just let His presence rest on you, and He doesn't have to say anything. You can physically feel His love saturating your entire being, and suddenly, He reveals His will. We all need time in His presence, or else we'll just act like everyone else in the world.

All of these types of experiences start with desire, and time spent seeking the Lord. After praying for a while before the start of a particular church service, I went out to sit on the platform and wait. As I was waiting for the service to begin, the Holy Spirit came upon me and directed my attention to a young man on the front row. When the Holy Spirit comes "upon" you like this, His presence is something that can clearly be felt. It is not just some mental thing as many believe. There's

Making Money With God

nothing else in the world like it. If you've never experienced this, keep reading. Let your hunger and faith will grow for such experiences.

After getting my attention, the Lord clearly said to me, "Tell that young man that *she* is not the one!" So after the service, I stopped the young man and repeated what God had to say. Well, his eyes lit up and he explained how he had been thinking about asking his college girlfriend to marry him. Then he told me that he "was already starting to feel that it might be the wrong thing to do," which is often the way the Lord leads. He already knew in his spirit, but God was nice enough to confirm it through someone else. We don't always sort things out in our spirits properly, especially when it comes to love. So, God offers confirmation. "Attraction" to the opposite sex is natural, but it does NOT equal God's will just because it happens. We must control our thoughts.

I share this event just to point out that this young man had been **diligently** asking God for direction, and I had also been waiting on the Lord to be used. I love being used by God, and it's eternal. So much of what we spend our time on will be totally forgotten, and we have very little time on this earth. God gave us both what we were asking for, just as He promised. But most people in the world, and even in the church, won't seek God like this, so they never experience much of anything from God. They go to church once or twice a week, maybe do some devotions, and that's about it. You must be hungrier for the things of God than that, if you're going to experience miracles.

In my travels to different churches, I've made it a habit to always honor the person in charge by asking permission to move in the gifts of the Spirit. God honors authority, and if the person in charge does not give that permission for some reason, which happens occasionally, then it is no longer my responsibility. The responsibility is all on the pastor if he says "no" to the Holy Spirit, unless God gives me further instructions.

In such situations, God has led me to catch certain people after the service, to deliver a word, or minister in some other way. On several occasions, I've written down a "word" from God and then made sure the intended "got the memo." I'm a real stickler for delivering what God sends me to give. The importance of one real word from God is unmatched, and it can drastically change a life. Paul said that such gifts will establish the believer(s). I've seen one "word" from God cause people to weep, repent, and even be physically healed.

I certainly don't blame pastors for being cautious about the use of spiritual gifts. The Bible warns us to judge such things. Some pastors have made me "prove" my ministry abilities before they would turn me loose on their congregations; but God has always stood with me. God doesn't seem to mind this type of testing when the pastor is not used to such things, and if in his heart he's really just trying to protect the sheep. I, too, am very cautious when someone tells me they have "something from God." There is no shortage of flaky people in the church, so it pays to check for legitimacy in the things of God.

If you haven't gotten it yet, "**diligent** seeking" of the Lord's face is the action that brings God's manifestations on the scene. But also, corporate cooperation can determine the level of God's power in church. I've been places where the expectancy is so great you can literally feel their faith pulling on your anointing. But, then, other places seem like your trying to pray for a door knob to come to life. Do you remember that Jesus found it difficult to minister in some towns, because of their unbelief? Unbelief comes from hearing, just like faith does. Only, it's hearing the wrong thing.

Just plain ole normal church doesn't usually make supernatural things happen. You must "press in" if you want miracles. Many churches are just like watching the same movie every week. You know exactly what's going to happen before it does. I don't see how God can stand it. Surely, He must be bored to tears.

Miracles don't just fall to the ground like ripe cherries. Are you willing to dig a hole through a roof to get to Jesus, like the guy in the Bible? Would you climb a tree to be noticed, or press through a crowd of naysayers, calling out to Jesus like the blind man did? Will you go sit in a closet until God speaks to you, no matter how long it takes? If you want a miracle, you have to pursue it with everything within you; and don't take "no," or religious excuses, for an answer.

If churches won't teach or allow God's gifts to operate, even if God is there trying to do something, not much will happen. Some pastors "think" they're protecting the sheep this way, but if they persist in stopping the legitimate "gifts of the Spirit," they're only keeping the sheep from being touched by their Savior. Most pastors don't knowingly stop the gifts, but by wrong teaching, or a lack of encouraging the

Making Money With God

gifts, they stop them by default. The church is severely short changed when the gifts are not allowed. Talking and teaching simply won't solve everything. Jesus proved this many times by backing up His sermons with action.

Wouldn't you love for an occasional Sunday morning service to end with a powerful move of God, instead of a mad dash for the buffet line? God will not usually override the pastor's authority in a church. He will not force a church to operate in the gifts of the Spirit, if the pastor thinks it's distasteful. They must be thoroughly desired, and allowed by the leadership.

The common disclaimer, "Well, God can do whatever He wants here," is not sufficient if the leadership doesn't really believe in, or do what it takes to "stir up," the gifts. No one will have faith for the "gifts," if they're not taught properly, and encouraged. Some readers are being stirred by just reading the few experiences in this book. That's good. We can't believe for something we don't know about.

God ALWAYS wants to help people and set them free, but it's not going to happen in a church that doesn't know anything about the supernatural. The formula of "Get them in; give them a quick touchy/feely sermonette; get their money; and get them out within an hour," might bring people who like to get church over with as soon as possible, but it won't bring God's presence on the scene. But, the service doesn't have to be hours long though, either. There must be a strong hunger for God if you want miracles, and time for the Holy Spirit to work. It's okay to have a "program," as long as you don't go by it. Hunger comes by hearing, too.

We should be sensitive to God's desires in a service. And we don't have to "keep the service moving" with constant talking and fill, as if we're on the radio. It's okay to slow down, relax, and listen to God. He might do a miracle right in your midst, and you won't even have to preach your wonderful sermon. The people will flock to the altars, and for the next service, you'll have standing room only. I've seen this very thing happen.

Some churches have their services planned out weeks, months, and even years in advance. I just don't get that at all. It's a sure way to keep God out of the service. Sometimes I don't know what God wants to do until I'm in the middle of a service, or at the end. If He told me in advance, I would probably mess it up with my own planning. We should "go with the flow."

I'm not really going to try and build a case, or argue with the naysayers. If someone doesn't want to have literal communion with God, or benefit from the gifts of the Spirit, no one is going to make them. But, if you want God, don't let skewed religion block you from entering in when the Bible is chockfull of examples of God leading and speaking to those who seek Him. "He never changes!" Religion has always been God's greatest enemy.

God has spoken to me concerning many various things, from money issues, to world events, and His communication has come in a variety of forms, just as it did in the Bible. His "still small voice," is probably the way I hear Him the most, but He may develop something different in you. Some Christians see visions or dreams quite often, and these visions show them how to minister in a certain situation. Jesus operated that way, but it is only one form of God's leading.

When I speak in churches, God often gives me "words of knowledge" (little bits of information) concerning illnesses, problems, or other needs that people have in the congregation. This is one of the gifts of the Holy Spirit that is listed in I Cor. 12, for the use of blessing people. When God reveals someone's sickness to a minister, or another person, faith is sparked in the sick person because they know that God really cares, and healing often occurs simultaneously. "Words of knowledge" aren't always about sickness though, they can be about anything.

The Lord has given me "words" for people about real estate deals, direction in mission work, where to go next, why they're not being healed, money problems, and many other things. Once in New Zealand, following a church service, a teenager came to me for prayer about reoccurring nightmares. As soon as he said the word "nightmares," within my spirit I heard the Lord say, "Harry Potter books." When I asked him about the books, his mother, who was standing next to him, hung her head shamefully and said, "The books are mine." She then repented and promised to get rid of the books. We prayed and the nightmares stopped. God knows the answer to every problem. Why don't you tap in?

We must have God's voice and power. The teachings that imply that the true gifts of the Spirit are just "natural gifts," are misleading. You don't get a "word of wisdom" by going to school, or earning a

Making Money With God

degree. There's nothing wrong with that, but a "word of wisdom" comes straight from God, to you, instantly. All of the spiritual gifts are exactly that, "spiritual gifts." That means they're "supernatural," not natural. "Except no substitutes," or you'll miss many of the things that God has for you.

There's no telling how many "pats on the back" the desperate alcoholic receives in most churches, but no real help. Cancer victims often get plenty of "prayer chain" type prayer, but there's seldom enough power in the whole church to even stop a head cold, much less something deadly. When are we going to really believe that God is with us?

If desperate people want a real miracle, God has to try and send them some place they've never been before, to accomplish something that should be available in any church. But even then, they usually won't go. Are you willing to follow God for the kind of power Jesus had? Are you that hungry? Do you think Jesus was kidding when He said we could do the same works He did? I'm sharing these things so you'll start to get a sense for hearing, and the hunger necessary for seeking God. And I'm hoping some of the pastors reading along will determine to be the powerful men God wants them to be. Don't settle for just a sermon and a good offering. Set people free, rescue hostages, deliver the captives, and be a hero!

If I desperately needed a miracle and I didn't have the faith necessary myself, I would drive city to city and knock on doors until I found someone with real miracle faith. It all depends on how bad you want something. And if you're not interested, don't worry; you won't be bothered by unwanted miracles.

When I receive a "word of knowledge," I usually hear it, but I know others who actually "feel" the sickness in their own bodies. Sometimes God will speak to you with a reoccurring thought. Or, something or someone just keeps coming to mind, and maybe you're troubled in your spirit when you think of that person. God is trying to get you to pray for that person, or even contact them. You might be meditating on something, and then a particular thought, idea, or fact, just starts to solidify in your mind.

Suddenly, you know the answer, or have information you didn't have a few minutes ago. These are all ways that God speaks, imparts, or leads, and there are other ways as well. God has often confirmed things for me with verses from the Bible, especially in trading. I've been

A. Bruce Wells

amazed many times by how He's placed a verse right before me that mentions the very item He had already put in my spirit to trade.

A few days ago, I wrote in a previous chapter of an example concerning the buying and selling of gold. Well, I didn't just choose that situation at random. God had been bringing gold before me for several days, and the prices used in the example, were real prices for that day. Well, guess what: This is the end of February, 2009, and gold went all the way up to $1,000 per ounce since I wrote that example just less than two weeks ago. Too bad you didn't have my book then, but there's always something new coming up and God knows what it is. A move like that would gross a $10,000 profit on just one contract. Gold then immediately sold off to around $950.

One of the most common ways that God speaks to me, especially concerning trading or investing, is through what I call ***the highlighting effect***. In other words, I'll hear something, or see something from just everyday things, and God will make it stand out, like something highlighted, or in **bold**, *italicized* type.

For instance, I might hear someone on a financial TV show say something like, "Now is the time to buy soy beans," and their words would seem to almost jump out and pierce my spirit. People say such things all the time, and normally it wouldn't mean anything to me, but God has a way of making certain things sound like they're coming from Him, even though He's using someone else's words. He will often confirm these things through another source, as well. I've had God do this with billboards, bumper stickers, words from sermons, and as most Christians should be able to relate, verses from the Bible.

I even experienced this once while I was playing a card game about trading commodities called *PITT.* At the end of our very first round, I ended up with all the "cocoa" cards and won that round. This wouldn't mean anything normally, but at this particular time, I had the strongest sense that this was not just a coincidence. Sure enough, the cocoa market surged the next few days due to a shortage in Africa. It's amazing what God can use to speak, if you're tuned in.

On another occasion, I was really praying about buying a particular stock that had caught my attention. It was a financial stock going by the symbol, GROW, and it was trading below $10 per share. The more I prayed, the more I felt good about the stock, but I was still asking God to speak to me about it. Well, while riding in my car, and just seconds

Making Money With God

after asking God if I should buy GROW or not, I turned on the radio to a Christian station and instantly some preacher shouted out, "IT'S TIME TO *GROW* UP," and I knew I had my answer. Leadings don't get much clearer than that, so I headed home and bought a thousand shares. The stock went way up, thank you Jesus.

If "insider trading" was legal, and the President of Toyota called you personally and said, "We're getting ready to buy millions of our own shares, and the price is going to go up dramatically;" would you know what to do? I know what I would do. Well, guess what: God knows about every company, and commodity on the planet, and it is absolutely "legal" when He tells you. So what are you waiting for?

As I said before, I'm careful to avoid trying to make these things happen, because that's a quick door to deception. Some seemingly coincidental things might actually be coincidental, or even demonic. But, when it's God, there are usually several things working at once, such as your inward witness, and other confirming signs.

Many Christians don't believe in coincidence. They proudly announce, "Nothing happens by coincidence because God plans everything!" But, the Bible plainly states that "time and chance happens to all," Ec. 9:11. Even Jesus said that the priest, in the story of the Good Samaritan, came along "*by chance.*" Luke 10:31 Yes, you can be fooled or deceived if you don't learn to discern when God is in something, or not, and He doesn't cause or plan everything. We still have free will.

I recently heard a song claiming that God tells each lightening bolt where to go. That one verse explains much of the church's confusion about God, and His will. While the song's intention was to honor God, it is totally **not true** that He tells every lightening bolt where to go, or that He arranges everything else that happens in our lives. We have choices to make, and lightening follows the path of least resistance. God "can" direct a lightening bolt, but they're usually just randomly discharged due to atmospheric conditions. In other words, God didn't target, or kill, everyone who has ever been struck by lightening. Nor did He ordain the bad things that might be happening in your life.

One example of God "highlighting" a verse for me happened years ago as I was seeking the Lord about my next trade. I had gone for several weeks without hearing anything, but I kept praying. My motto is: "If you don't hear anything, don't do anything;" so I kept waiting. Finally, one morning I got up very early to seek the Lord. After waiting a bit,

He spoke to me in that "still small voice" and said, "Go read Nahum, chapter one."

You should note that early morning is a good time for "hearing," before the day gets too busy. Jesus made a habit of getting up very early, and He led a pretty successful life. But let me say this again, so you don't get discouraged. Hearing will take *practice*.

When I read down to verse 13 of chapter 1 in Nahum, I saw the words, "I will break your *bonds* asunder (King James version)" and those words just jumped off the page as if they were electronically amplified. What did this mean? Well, I had been watching the T-Bond market because the price of Treasury Bonds had climbed abnormally high. I knew this because I regularly check all the markets purposely, looking for prices that are out of line. This will often be an opportunity. Eventually they will snap back into place and this makes it very easy to predict the direction. Figuring out "when," is the hard part.

So, God was nice enough to tell me, with this one piece of a verse, that the bond market was about to be cut down in price. And exactly that happened, starting 2 days later. In fact, it kept going down for quite some time, and with commodities, you can make just as much money when the price goes down as you can when it goes up. You just have to tell your broker the direction you're betting on.

When you're new at this, as you're trying to discern the difference between your thoughts and God's, quite often you'll find yourself asking, "God, is that you, or is that me?" God often taps in on the inner voice of your own thought process, so it can easily sound like "your" thought because He's using your inner voice. But, as you go, and grow, you'll learn when it's Him, or when it's just you. It will have a distinguishable feel to it.

Sometimes, God waits until you're thinking about something totally unrelated so you'll see the contrast when His thought is inserted. This will help you realize that it is not your own thought. The Lord does this a lot with me. I'll be praying about my family, a friend, or something personal, and suddenly, here comes this strong thought about something in the Middle East, or a political problem, or a pastor who's in trouble, and maybe God wants me to go help him.

The other day, I was taking down some window blinds and when I got to the third window, I had this thought that I didn't have before. The thought was, "check for spiders first," but I totally assumed it was

Making Money With God

just my thinking because my mind was already on the blinds. Well, just to be safe, I checked anyway, and sure enough, there was a huge brown spider in the corner, which can be pretty dangerous in Florida. Then it occurred to me, I didn't have that thought at the first or second windows, so it must have been the Lord. I decided that I must be a little out of tune since I couldn't tell the difference. Prayer, fasting, and time in the Word, are the answers to this problem.

You should try and remember the feelings and patterns of your mistakes for comparison to the times that you discern correctly. Did it really "click" with your spirit? Or was it just dry? Were you trying to help it along, or did it have a certain strength or staying power of its own? Often, when it's God, the thought will just seem right to you, and that feeling will linger a bit. Again, there is a distinct "feel" that you'll learn to recognize when God is speaking, and eventually you'll be able to weed out your own wishful thinking, or other thoughts or imaginations. This is why they had the "school of the prophets" in the OT. They were learning to hear God, too.

Once, after making a mistake discerning something, God helped me by "highlighting" a billboard phrase for me. The billboard was about buckling your seat belt, and the catch phrase was, *Make it click!*" God was trying to tell me, "Be certain that a thought or leading is from God before you act." "Make it click!"

I often check myself by repeating what I believe I'm hearing, to myself. If it's wrong, I can usually feel God checking me in my spirit, and it just doesn't "feel" right. But if it's right, that sense only grows, or continues. If that doesn't make sense to you now, someday it will. Also, I'm always asking God to keep me from mistakes when I'm operating in spiritual gifts. If you'll stay humble, He will protect you. It's when we get proud or try to show off, or try to be spiritual, that mistakes are easily made.

When you start thinking, "these people just don't realize how spiritual I am," it's time to go and flog yourself, or put on some sackcloth and ashes. Do us all a favor and don't let us find out "how spiritual you really are." Just be thankful that God is willing to use any of us.

Recently, I was having dinner out with my wife when she mentioned that the pregnant wife of her nephew was going to have a sonogram to see if their baby was a boy or girl. As soon as she said that, a strong feeling that it was a boy came over me. But before I spoke, I repeated

A. Bruce Wells

my answer to myself a couple of times, to see if it "felt" true. Each time, there was no "check" in my spirit, or sense that I was making a mistake, and it just "felt" right. God will tell you if you want to know, especially if you want to maintain integrity and humility. I said to my wife, "I can tell you what the baby is right now."

Well, a week later, my wife called me and said, "You were right, they had an ultrasound and it's a boy!" So I basked in the moment because, as any minister knows, it's rare to receive any spiritual acclaim from your wife. She knows all the dumb things you do at home, when you're not under the anointing. In ministry, it's pretty common to only get credit from those who don't know you. Jesus had the same problem, even though He never did dumb things at home, like the rest of us.

When God first spoke to Samuel, the boy didn't know that it was God speaking. It took some instruction and he soon learned to recognize God's voice. You may not be called to be a prophet, but you can still learn to recognize God's voice, just like any other voice you might identify on the telephone by hearing only. Jeremiah had to learn to interpret and discern the things that God was showing him in visions and thoughts. There is always the possibility of interpreting or hearing amiss. Plus, if you have some bad theology lurking in your mind, which is probable, you might read your faulty doctrine into whatever God has shown you, and then miss the whole thing. I've seen many do exactly that.

I know of someone who knew through prayer and revelation that a bad hurricane was coming to New Orleans (Katrina). But, this same person then interpreted it as some kind of "judgment." It is common for someone to get a little piece of information from God, and then read in a bunch of other stuff because of their brand of Christianity, which may have a wrong focus. So, instead of this revelation just being a "warning" that a hurricane was coming, this guy made it into something that God was sending out of anger, which is very doubtful. Hurricanes have been coming to that area for thousands of years, and the New Orleans mayor, and those in congress, had been warned about their levees many times before. That whole disaster should have been avoided.

If you build a city next to the ocean, below sea level, and in a common hurricane lane; sooner of later, you're going to get "judged." Jesus referred to this as foolishly "building on sand" before the storm comes. There will always be storms, but don't accuse God of judging you

Making Money With God

if you build you house on the side of an active volcano; or on a hill side where mud slides are common. Christians are quick to call any disaster that happens, "the judgment of God," especially when it's happening to someone else. They usually don't know what they're talking about.

The statement I'm about to make will probably sound haughty, elitist, or negative, but I don't say it for any of those reasons. I'm saying it simply because it's true, and it might motivate you to seek truth and answers that are real.

Here it is: After almost 30 years of ministry, I have found that most all Christians are either partially wrong, or totally wrong, about any given subject you can think of concerning the Bible. And even though many give a strong appearance of being right, they rarely are. From healing, faith, power, or money; to government, authority, law, grace, judgment, miracles, and/or literally anything else you could name from the Bible, church people seldom know theologically, doctrinally, or experientially, what they're talking about. Deception, ignorance, and religion, are extremely powerful forces in the church, and these forces keep God's people in mental prisons even though they are positive that they're knowledgeable about God and His word.

This huge problem comes from laziness and the fundamentally wrong way that Christians are taught to study the Bible, which we won't really get into right now. Very few Christians know anything about "rightly dividing" the Word, or even where one covenant stops and the other begins, or why. They constantly mix both covenants together while not even realizing the basic differences in the covenants, or what God is actually saying in the passage they're reading, or to whom it is even addressed.

We take things that were addressed to other cultures, hundreds of years before the cross, and apply them to the church. And then we take the things that apply to today's church, and say that they don't apply, anymore. And this is often from the leadership, so it's no wonder that the sheep are constantly confused.

Most of us don't even realize that Jesus' ministry was totally governed by the Old Covenant, which can really be confusing when one starts wondering why Jesus practiced or endorsed the Law in certain situations. But then Paul teaches that we shouldn't practice the Law, so who is right? Well, the simple answer is that New Covenant actually starts at the Resurrection, and not at the beginning of Matthew. No one taught me this for years after I was saved, and I was studying and going to meetings daily. This one little piece of information changed everything for me.

Of course, most readers will think that the things I just said don't really apply to them, but just the sheer lack of abundance and victory in the church is proof enough that it probably does. Is your life full of victory and joy, or are you waiting for some future "breakthrough," like most Christians? Be honest, or continue to be deceived. The "breakthrough" you really need is in your thinking. Any hope of a "future move of God" that will provide something for you that is not available now, is probable evidence that you don't know what He's already done at the cross. (You should read that last sentence again.)

Do this: Ask God to identify any and all wrong thinking in your mind. Much of it will be based on religion and half truths, or partially quoted verses. And don't be surprised when it turns out to be stuff that you thought was absolutely correct.

God will reveal the lies (strongholds) that are registered in your mind one at a time, if you want Him to. He won't give it to you all at once because your brain might explode. But, "little by little," He'll help you "possess the land (your mind)," if you're open to His help. Many won't ask God to do this because they're afraid He actually will, and they don't want to know. Or, they're positive they're right about everything now. It takes work to change your thinking, but it's the only lasting way out of your troubles.

ABOUT SHORTING THE MARKET

As mentioned before, when the DOW keeps going down, like it did after the last election, and *because* of the last election, it is possible to "short" the whole DOW index and make just as much money as it goes down, proportionally, as you would if it was going up. Along with many other items and indexes, The DOW index is traded on the commodities market just like you would buy gold or wheat. You only have to choose the right direction.

(When I point out that the "last election" negatively affected the DOW, I say this for no other reason than this always happens when someone with a "Liberal-Socialist" philosophy is elected. Wealthy people are usually very savvy and heavily invested in the stock market, and they know that "big spending, big government, and liberal decision making" is always bad for the economy, so they get out. History has proven this time and again. Such a stock market exodus might last for months.)

If someone owns just one DOW futures contract, and the market moves in the direction they chose, either up or down, that person would make $10 for each point. The various "point values" for each commodity are listed on a number of websites, along with the margins (cost for each contract), or they can be found out from any good broker. 100 points would be worth $1,000, if you chose the right direction. Today, the DOW dropped 262 points, which would be a profit of $2,620 for every one who owned a "short" contract. When it hits a bottom, the smart money will simply reverse their orders and take a "long" (up) position. People, who learn to do this, can take advantage of the market if it's going up or down, while everyone else is crying.

Anyone shorting (bet on it going down) the market, on or before Inauguration Day of 2009, would be way ahead now. Much of the country is still running for cover. Often, you can make money faster when markets go down than when they go up, simply because they usually fall faster due to fear. I've learned to simply not care if prices are going up or down for any particular commodity. I just want to know from the Holy Spirit which direction is correct for me to ride. But, most investors only think in terms of making money when the market is going up. They are greatly limited in a bear market.

NEVER get into something and then start asking God to make it go the direction that you want. **Always find out, beforehand**, the direction that it is already bound to go due to many contributing forces. You should read that again. You may think you have the faith to move the markets of the world, but you probably don't. It is much easier to just go with the flow of a river, than it is to try and reverse the whole course of the river. Have you ever tried to push water up hill?

There are probably just as many people praying for any given market to go the opposite of what you want, anyway. In trading, or in life, when you find that you're wrong about something, just stop and go the other way! Don't keep trying to surf from the beach out to the ocean when the waves are going the other way. How dumb is that?

Wait for the bus that's going where you want to go. Don't just jump on any bus and then try to grab the steering wheel because you got on the wrong bus. I've seen Christians do this with many impetuous decisions. And while we're talking about buses, you should know that commodities make regularly scheduled stops, just like the bus line. So if you miss a move. Don't chase it or panic; wait on God. He may tell you to run to the next stop for entry, or He may tell you to just wait until it comes around again, and it will. Or He may just tell you to forget it and start looking for something else.

Have you ever had God speak a verse to you, or speak through a verse while you're just reading along? Have you ever been corrected, or encouraged this way. Well, God will speak to you about money matters too, if you'll adjust your faith that way and seek Him for specific information concerning investments. I've gotten direction hundreds of times this way. You'll be surprised at how many verses God can use to speak to you concerning trading.

I've received direction through verses about cattle, wheat, soy beans, gold, bonds, silver, barley, lumber and many others, all telling me what to do next. But, this happens because I'm *diligently* (key word) seeking the Lord and asking Him for direction. One day, my son and I were praying about the next move in the market and the Lord led me to Revelation 3:18 where Jesus said, "I advise you to buy gold," and the Holy Spirit "highlighted" that part of the verse for me. The gold market then moved up about $100 per ounce; not a small move at all.

I meditate on the verses that promise this type of direction, such as John 16:13, where Jesus promised that the Holy Spirit would "show us things to come." You should think about the power of that verse for a while. The Holy Spirit will literally show you the future if you'll believe, and if you desire, even concerning money making prospects. How do you think God made Abraham rich? Wealth didn't just fall out of heaven for him. God "led" Abraham in trading and making business deals. When Peter needed tax money, it didn't drop out of heaven. Jesus told him where to go, and how to get it; and He knows where the money is that you need.

When God led me a thousand miles to buy that investment property, I didn't realize it at the time, but He was actually showing me the future because He knew that property would increase in value and yield a huge profit. When God led me to Nahum chapter 1, He was showing me the short term "future" of T-bonds.

Making Money With God

Daniel knew the future of Egypt because God gave him the interpretation of the King's dream. He then prepared to save the people and make a profit at the same time. God often arranges win-win situations that are beneficial to everyone involved. When you know the future of any financial market, you can easily make money. I find it interesting that commodities are also called, "futures!" We just have to find out the price direction from God, and remember, He knows everything.

A huge stumbling block for most of us today is; we think that God was more active, more helpful, more powerful, and easier to contact, in Daniel's day than now. We read those stories like they're only ancient history and such things will never happen again. But, the truth is, GOD IS MUCH MORE EASILY ACCESSED TODAY, AND WE HAVE "BETTER PROMISES" THAN DANIEL EVER DREAMED OF! (Pun intended) You have been made the very "righteousness of God," and you stand before Him as pure and holy as Jesus Himself, with God living inside you! Daniel never had such a blessing.

When you're watching a parade from the street level, you can only see the portion of the parade that is right in front of you. But, if you move to a very high elevation, you can see the whole parade from the beginning to the end. You know what's coming next while the people on the ground only know what is happening right in front of them. This is what God is able to do in the realm of time, and He'll share it with you. Sometimes He will broadcast information to those who have ears to hear. Have you ever noticed how sometimes, a number of preachers will all preaching on the same subject at the same time? It's because that subject is "in the air."

Think about this for a moment: There are invisible radio waves all around you even as you're reading this, and many things are being said. But, unless you're "tuned in," you can't hear what's being said even though the existence of these voices are as real as the air your breathing. Well, God is not an impersonal radio broadcast, but He is constantly trying to warn, help, direct, and bless people. But, hearing His warnings or directions, takes a little bit of doing on our part. We must learn to tune in and focus. We must consciously pay attention by faith!

Do you remember how all the students from The School of the Prophets knew that Elijah was going to be taken up? How did they all know this at the same time? They knew because it was in the air, and because God was broadcasting. Do you remember how Jesus was often upset because His people didn't know what was going on spiritually? Jesus expected them to be "tuned in," like He was. But they were usually "dull of hearing." Well, something "dull" can be sharpened, and it is our job is to stay sharp, if we're going to hear God.

Those who are tuned into God can know what people are really like on the inside. Those who are "tuned in" are amazed when voters fall for the false promises and dishonesty of smiling politicians. Out-of-tune voters make faulty decisions simply because someone looks good on the outside, and says what they want to hear. But, those who are "tuned in" will have a feel for honesty and good character, or the absence of it. If you are honest, you'll be good at judging character, and you'll sense when something is wrong. Don't ignore these feelings, or get caught up in wishful thinking. Finely tuned sensitivity can keep you out of a lot of trouble.

If all of America was standing before God and listening to His council, our country wouldn't be so messed up due to the election of ungodly people who simply know how to lie convincingly. We wouldn't have to say later, "Ooops, we sure blew it by voting for that man, or woman." That goes for the rest of the world, too. The same is true in all relationships, business and personal.

Forgive me for saying so much about politics, but "political authority" is only the means by which an office holder asserts his or her brand of morality. There is no such thing as "separating" this from "the state," so Christians should be very much involved. "Legislating morality," is the definition of politics.

No real Christian should ever be deceived by a politician or the likes of a Bernie Madoff. God is living on the inside of those who have been born again. Many of those who followed Madoff were nice people, but they simply weren't spending time with God, and I'm not talking about just going to church. It's only when we override our inward witness, or our consciences, that we get deceived and actually talk ourselves into doing the wrong thing. Then once we've *conned* ourselves, we start trying to *con*vince others. That's exactly what the Madoff crowd did with each other; and the same thing is happening everyday in congress as men and women push expensive, harmful legislation.

I'm hammering this issue because Christians, even seasoned ones, can be very gullible. I've seen Christians who, after listening to me warn them for years about believing every goofy scheme that comes along, turn around and give all their investment money to phony ministers and charlatans who promised great returns while claiming they were sent from God. Here's a great clue: If they're legitimate, and they really know what they're doing, they shouldn't need "your" money.

It's good to have faith, and to be a believer, but DON'T BELIEVE EVERYTHING that comes along! Ninety nine out of a hundred money making schemes you'll hear among Christians, are a waste of time and money. And I'm being conservative about that estimate. Some are even well intentioned, but everyone is still going to lose.

Again, Christians run to every "this is going to finance the end-time-harvest" thing that comes along, and then a year later, they're pushing something else. I wish I had a dollar for every time I've heard the "But this one is really different," pitch. If you really want to "finance the end time harvest," go buy some gospel tracts and start leading people to Christ! Those, who are always raising money, never seem to get enough to actually do it. They scare more souls away than they ever bring in.

Harvesting souls has never been a "money problem" anyway. It has always been **A LABOR PROBLEM!** Jesus even commanded us to pray for laborers. Whenever God has told me to go anywhere in the world, the money always showed up as I was making the arrangements. If you're really "sent," God, as a good employer, will provide. If you just "went," like so many do, you'll have to raise your own money. Read the revivals in the New Testament. They were always started with a willing mouths and miracle power. The money came later.

Another great verse that I like to meditate and appropriate for trading is Isaiah 42:9. God said, "Behold, the former things are come to pass and new things do I declare: **before they spring forth, I will tell you of them**." I love this verse! Think about what God is literally saying! BEFORE IT HAPPENS, I WILL TELL YOU WHAT IS GOING TO HAPPEN! Isn't that great! Why would He say this if He didn't mean it? God has encouraged me with this verse many times when I was wondering what to do next. If you'll believe, God will tell you the future, too. If you'll listen, God will put you in the right place, at the right time. But you must be ready and looking, or you could miss it.

Start practicing your ability to hear God. Jesus said, "My sheep **HEAR** my voice." That's you! Start reciting that verse while expecting it to be true. Ask God to teach you to hear! He wants you to hear clearly, even more than you want it!

Practice, practice, practice! Ask God what your preacher is going to preach on this Sunday; then get quiet and listen, and see if you get it right. Ask Him who is calling before you look at the caller ID. Anymore, I almost always know who's calling me before I answer, without looking. I had "caller ID" before it was even invented. God even helps me when I'm watching Jeopardy. My wife gets upset because I'll often call out the answer for Final Jeopardy before they even read the clue. I did that twice in a row this week. Am I that smart? No, but the Holy Spirit is. There's nothing wrong with having fun as you're learning.

Just for fun, God told me who was going to win the last Superbowl, days before it was played. My family didn't believe that I had actually heard the Lord when my underdog team was way behind in the first quarter. But, vindication came in the second half as the team of my prediction (really God's) moved way ahead. Of course I gloated for several days.

"Brother Bruce! You didn't really gloat, did you? You should be giving God the glory!" Will you relax? God knows very well that I understand how pitiful I am without Him. He likes to exalt his children, though, just like you do. He did this with many people in the Bible. Who is more excited about a touch down; the one who scored it, or the father who's sitting in the stands?" Quit being so religious, and enjoy your relationship with God. This will actually help you hear Him, better.

You can consciously look inside yourself and focus on listening to the Holy Spirit. A well known minister from the 1950's once said. "Looking into the spiritual realm is like going to the circus when I was a child. I didn't have enough money to get in, but I could pull myself up enough to see over the fence. By faith, one can do the same thing with God. You can consciously pull yourself up to look into the spiritual realm."

Some Christians would have a problem with that statement, but I've found it to be very true. Sometimes God will give you things you're not even looking for, or trying to get, but it is also true that you can pull things out of Him, by faith. The woman with the "issue of blood" did exactly that in Luke chapter 8.

I know of a couple of preachers who used to practice hearing God by hiding from one another in a large city. Then they would try to find

Making Money With God

each other by listening to God. They got to be pretty good at it, too. I suggest starting in a mall or something smaller, first. Then try a whole city, if this interests you.

One day, before cell phones, I missed a rendezvous with some friends of mine who were going somewhere to win souls, but they hadn't told me where. So, remembering the two preachers just mentioned, I asked God to tell me where my soul-winning friends were headed. He quietly whispered the name of a high school that was all the way across town. My friends were amazed when they arrived and I was already there passing out tracts in the school parking lot. Once again, God knows everything! Our job is to learn to hear.

I hope these things are wetting your appetite, and getting you interested in walking and talking with God daily. If we could ever get this reality in our lives, we would never have to worry about anything, or ever be at a loss for the right wisdom or instruction at any given moment. **We should have MORE wisdom than Solomon!** Jesus said, "A greater one than Solomon is here." And now He's inside us! Matt. 12:42 The Bible also says, "Jesus has been made unto us, wisdom..." I Cor. 1:30

If you lose your job, Jesus can tell you exactly what to do next. Is your child rebellious and angry? God can tell you why, and what to do. Are you not being healed of something? The Holy Spirit can tell you exactly why. Do you want to make your spouse really happy? Ask God what to do for them. He knows everything, from where you should go to church, to who you should marry. He knows where you should work, who you should hang out with, what's true and not true, which fish has gold in its mouth, who NOT to trust, what the stock market is going to do, and anything else you could possibly need. So start learning to hear!

One of the earliest experiences I had hearing the Lord's voice, was after I had literally put myself in a closet and determined that I wasn't coming out until I heard God speak. I had heard others say that God had told them this or that, so I was determined to have that for myself. I was prepared to stay in that closet for days, but it only took an hour or so before the Lord spoke to me.

But, just before He spoke, I had an interesting experience that I had never heard of, but have since heard others speak of. I had felt God's presence before, but this time, as His presence came into the closet, the little room filled with a wonderful fragrance of roses. It was just as if someone had opened the door and sprayed air freshener in, except it was much fresher, and more real. Shortly after that, the "word of the Lord" came to me. To my surprise, God took the opportunity to give me some ministry instructions. He actually spoke someone's name and told me to go see this person, who was in jail. He also told me how to minister to this guy.

Long story short, this fellow, who had shot at a policeman in an attempt to get the policeman to kill him (suicide), prayed with me to be saved. He was then miraculously released the next week on bond, which another Christian paid, and he went home and led his whole family to the Lord. Then they all started going to church the same week. Not a bad harvest for one little jail visit. I learned, right then and there, that listening to God can really produce some fruit. We should all try it, instead of just plugging along like we usually do, with minimal results. Listening to God can bless us in every realm of life. God can show you who is ripe, and who isn't.

One last point on hearing God; and even though this might make some people angry, I have to say it. You won't have the full advantage that God wants you to have if I don't mention this.

Are you ready? This is it: I didn't start hearing God's voice until after I received the baptism in the Holy Ghost and started praying in tongues. You, or your church, may not agree with this, but I'm just telling you how it was with me. You can believe or do whatever you want, but it was after I started praying in tongues that I started hearing God's voice, and I had been saved for 3 years before that. The baptism in the Holy Spirit came later and was definitely a separate experience from when I was born again, as it was for the people in Acts chapter 8, and the first eleven disciples. They were born again when Jesus breathed on them, but filled with the Holy Spirit sometime later.

Nothing like hearing God, or moving in the "gifts," ever happened to me during that first 3 year period of my salvation. I had some revelations through reading the Bible and listening to some teachings, but nothing as powerful as the experiences we read about in the NT. Experiences like Phillip had, such as when God told him to chase that chariot (Acts 8:29), or when Ananias was given specific directions to find the house where Paul was and pray for him (Acts 9:10 & 11), were **NOT** happening to me before I started praying in tongues.

Making Money With God

Actually, the first time I heard God's voice, was the very first time I really prayed in tongues out loud. I had felt God's presence before, and even sensed His leading, but I never actually heard His voice until after the tongues experience. And let me clarify that I'm not talking about the tongues used to give a prophetic message in a service, or the tongues used to speak to someone of another country, which are also very legitimate gifts. But, I'm speaking of the tongues that every Christian can have for their own personal prayer time, as Paul taught in I Corinthians 14. Don't read I Cor. 14 in light of what you've been taught, or while trying to prove a pre-conceived opinion. Read it to see what it actually says. It will bless you if you do.

Often, when I'm praying in tongues, the wisdom or answers I need for ministry or trading, just come right up out of my spirit. And when I don't know what to do, or feel that I have anything to offer, praying in tongues will strengthen my faith and restore my zeal, as it says in Jude. If everyone prayed in tongues for just an hour before church, the whole world would probably be saved by now. But, we just keep doing our own thing instead of letting God reveal His plan, and His thing. After their training period, Jesus told his men to do NOTHING, until they had this power.

I know there are people who have heard God without tongues, but it is much more frequent for those who spend time praying in tongues. This is a gift to help us be more tuned in and conditioned for ministry. It's God's idea, not mine. And the gifts of the Spirit are the very tools needed for most any type of ministry. Without the Holy Spirit, effectively, we're just another religion with a bunch of do's and don'ts.

My Jewish aunt asked for the baptism in the Holy Spirit after hearing about it, because she was hungry for something more than just religion. So, I went to her house to pray for her. Nothing happened right away after I prayed, but later, she woke up in the middle of the night speaking in tongues. Sometimes, our mind get's in the way of what God wants to do, so God helped her get started while sleeping. Personally, I'm interested in anything that God has available for our help, if it's truly scriptural. Maybe you don't need God's power, but I can't get along without it.

Again, it doesn't matter to me what you believe, or how you pray, but I'm just telling you what has worked for me, and how God has

A. Bruce Wells

led me. You can do whatever you want, but if you're hungry for more, there's nothing like be equipped with the same power Jesus had, which only comes from the Holy Spirit. I hope this has helped you.

CHAPTER 6

SHOULD CHRISTIANS HAVE WEALTH?

THIS DEBATE HAS CONTINUED for years, and probably more so in recent years since Christians now have much more access to teaching and information. But, as always, "tradition" (preconditioning) can be an enemy to the truth of God's Word. So please, be open minded to the information you're about to read. If our point is not scriptural, you can just throw it out.

You're going to hear dozens of good sounding opinions on this subject, which can lead to a truck load of confusion. But, if you really want to know where God stands on this, you're going to have to find out what is doctrinally provided in our redemption, and refuse traditional, religious thinking. You will have to rely on the immovable truth of redemption, regardless of how good and holy anyone's argument for the so called "blessings of being poor" may sound.

Religion can be very soothing and deceptive, like the serpent in the garden. If we were to take away all of the history of the demon inspired, counterfeit, religious institutions of the world, including the large portions of counterfeit Christianity, this whole issue of wealth for God's people wouldn't even be an "issue." It certainly isn't for the Jews.

Try to imagine what it would have been like if Jesus had redeemed Adam and Eve before there was any time for religion to be established, Satan's plan to keep us from really finding God, and truth. Just for a moment, let's pretend that Jesus' death and resurrection happened only one year after Adam and Eve sinned and were expelled from the "garden of abundance."

Then it would have been a simple matter of: *"Okay, your sin is forgiven, and you guys are restored to fellowship with God. Also, since you're* *now **redeemed**, you may leave this 'sweat of the brow and hard work situation,' which was the direct result of your sin; and you may return to the place of abundant provision and walking with God. Jesus' blood has made you totally righteous again, as you were before sin, and everything that goes with that righteousness is now restored."*

There's more to redemption than just that, but financial salvation, or "abundant provision," is really just that simple. It's only in the collective mind of the confused church that financial provision gets so difficult. It is false religion that has skewed the truth and made poverty seem like something holy and part of God's will, and this has greatly influenced real Christianity.

Several times in the Bible, God actually refers to poverty as "a curse," but most of the church didn't seem to get that memo. Take someone who was never influenced by church, let them read the Bible from cover to cover without listening to the common preaching of our day, and they would never come up with the idea that "God is against prosperity," or that "poverty and lack are actually blessings." It is only due to bad teaching from generations of religion, which has bled into much of the church, that we espouse such nonsense.

In years gone by, and even today, recognizing the dangers and temptations of having money, some have taken "vows of poverty" to protect themselves from temptation. And some have done this as an outward "show" of their alleged, inward holiness, but these measures were never the way that God wanted us to overcome sin. Unfortunately though, these ideas have bled into the real church in a variety of deceptive packages, as something that God thought up. Or, they're mistaken for something that leads to holiness, or humility, but they were never suggested, or ordered, by God.

Several years ago, we had plenty of what was called "the prosperity message;" and as with anything, some looked at this as being good news while others disdained and strongly criticized it. Some believe Christians are supposed to be wealthy, while others think they're not supposed to have much of anything in this life, but everything in the next.

Much of Christian leadership seems to fear the possibility of wealth for God's people because they are very aware of the dangers involved with the power of money. And these are very real dangers, but, does the existence of these problems mean that God has not redeemed us from poverty, or as Paul put it, "became poor that we might be made rich?"

Making Money With God

When redemption is thoroughly studied, it is obvious that God offered wealth in the atonement because man had abundant provision before the fall. But this may not be so clear to some, due to a constant feed of misinformation. Consider this: God is not in the habit of removing the temptations that confront us in any of the realms of life. His preference is for us to overcome them, rather than be kept hidden in a cave, or in lack.

Married men can be tempted by the availability of other women, but God doesn't remove all the other women from the planet just to keep some of us from temptation. And it would be just as silly to believe that He keeps us poor so that we don't ever have to deal with the problems of having money. No, He wants us to possess our souls, and learn how to be pure in any situation. Personally, I believe the problems of not having money, greatly out weigh the problems that come with having money. And I've been in both situations.

Unfortunately, this fear of money drives leadership to promote warnings in such a way that we're led to believe that having any degree of wealth is somewhat wicked. Consequently, many of us have this underlying thought that God is against prosperity even though, throughout the Bible, it has always been a reward for serving Him. I think this fear is often inbred and cultivated in our leaders by "their" leaders, and much of the preaching we hear stems from worry, and the fear of being corrupted in some way. They unconsciously make us believe that it is impossible to have wealth and good character at the same time. This concept is what I call "The *Either-Or* Syndrome," which will be discussed later.

As more food for thought, though, think about this: If God didn't want us to have abundance and success, why did He explain how to obtain these things so often in the Bible? Even under the Law, God told His people they would prosper, have success, and be given the power to **get wealth** (Deut. 8:18), if they obeyed His commandments. He promised this as a confirmation of their covenant.

So if the New Covenant is based on "better promises," should the promise of success and wealth be eliminated? Not in my thinking. But, many Christians believe we're better off struggling with poverty, lack, and fear. This is somehow supposed to build character, and let us know "how blessed we really are."

In Psalm 1, the Jews were promised success if they kept God's commandments. And also in Deut. chapter 28, as well as in chapter 8, they were promised wealth and success if they followed the instructions of the Law. Chapter 1 of Joshua promises prosperity and success for keeping the Law, as well. Then Jesus, in Matt. 6, promised that all the things that the Gentiles sought after, which would certainly include wealth, would be added to those who found God's kingdom and His righteousness. That would be everyone who has been "born again."

Then Paul taught us in Philippians 4:19 that God would meet our needs according to **HIS RICHES** in glory, not according to the poverty minded standards of the church. Have you really ever considered "HIS RICHES IN GLORY?" I'm guessing it's a bit more than what you're thinking. And of course, Paul also taught that Jesus became poor that we might be made rich, in II Cor. 8:9. Please note that this verse is found in a discourse on money, not in a discussion on "spiritual" riches. Even John, Jesus' closest disciple, prayed for believers to "prosper" and be in health (3 John 2). So again, if God didn't want us to prosper, why would He tell us how, and why would John pray for this vary thing? How many verses do we need before we'll take the hint?

I've heard many explain that Jesus condemned wealth when He told the disciples that it is very difficult for a man with "riches" to enter the kingdom of heaven. But, because Christians rarely examine the Word completely, or in context, they fail to realize that Jesus clarified this in the next verse, Mark 10:24.

After the disciples were amazed at such a statement, and then questioned Jesus about it, He added the word "**trust**" in His reply, saying, "It is difficult for those who **TRUST** in riches to enter the Kingdom," further illuminating His reasoning. The key word, of course, is "TRUST." Even poor people can trust in riches as they buy their lotto tickets, long for money, and envy the rich.

But again, because so many ministers lead by fear, they consequently deny the abundance that God has given us through redemption; and as a result, their small minded idea of God's provision has caused most of the church to live and labor under a spirit of poverty. If we can just scrape together a little bit of income, due to church teaching, we often feel that we're getting more than we deserve. Usually, people rarely earn more money than they "feel" they deserve. They subconsciously deny, or even sabotage, their own success due to roots of poor teaching and/ or strangled self worth.

Making Money With God

Obviously, Abraham, Isaac, Jacob, David, Solomon, and many other men of great wealth went to heaven. But these men trusted in God, not in their wealth. This same danger of trusting in the wrong thing exists in many other realms, including our works. It is not riches that condemn a rich man, but the state of his heart toward God. It is very easy for the rich to be prideful, arrogant, and callous because, for the moment, they don't need anyone.

Jesus knew that the rich young man of Mark 10 had a big problem trusting in his wealth. Abraham or David would have immediately given everything away, had God said to do so. God knew their hearts and it was not necessary to challenge them on this.

Another possible money problem verse, that is often misinterpreted, is 1st Tim. 6:9. It says, "But those who *want* to get rich fall into temptation and a snare…" So, there are many who condemn wealth by quoting this verse, but they seldom quote it with the true intended idea.

The phrase "want to get rich" doesn't really describe the intensity of the desire addressed in this verse. It is not a casual reference. Who in their right mind wouldn't prefer abundance over barely enough? This verse is actually talking about someone who is *consumed* with getting money as their number one goal. In other words, money is their god. Of course, there are multitudes caught in this trap, but Paul is warning the Christian to avoid this dangerous position.

The very next verse confirms the desire level of this point as it talks about the "*love* of money" and those who covet, or *long* for it. Again, this is a very different heart from the great men who loved God and had wealth, such as Abraham, Job, David, etc. The "*love*" of money is the root of all evil, not the money itself, 1st Tim. 6:10. This is a huge problem among the poor as well. **If money itself is evil, then we shouldn't have any at all!**

If you'll back up a bit in Timothy, you'll see that Paul writes about those who, according to the Greek text, use godliness as an access to gain. And again, many are guilty of this in the church world. Church is more of a career to them, than a calling. Or, they've discovered a way to lift offerings, or sell products that are more for profit than a help to the people. They're like the money changers in the outer court. They wear piety like a salesman wears a suit to influence a potential source of income. Once again, it is the condition of the heart, not the money.

Paul goes on to say that true godliness (contentment and a desire to please God) actually is a source of great gain, 1ˢᵗ Tim. 6:6. Of course, the religious mind will say that this is only spiritual gain, but again, the context is money. Godly men throughout the Bible prove this point again and again as God gave them power to get wealth. Some of this thinking will seem scary and strange to many Christians, but that's only because we've been heavily sedated with poverty minded church thinking. We've become like "institutionalized prisoners" who are actually afraid of freedom.

As mentioned above, "The Either-Or Syndrome" is a very common, subtle problem with most Christian reasoning and it usually leads to deception. When discussing prosperity, or any number of topics, you will often hear Christians say, "Well, I would *rather* have love, character, or humility, than _____;" you fill in the blank. Their preconditioned thinking tells them that they can't have *all* these things because they don't deserve an abundance of blessings.

In their minds, this would be too much like getting ALL of the presents under the Christmas tree. But, in God's world, **ALL** of the presents **ARE** for everyone! There is NO shortage of blessings, or a limited gift budget! It really takes some doing to expand our thinking into believing that God wants to give us way more than we probably want. The road block of "limiting Him" by what we believe we deserve, is not so easily overcome.

Christians believe, unconsciously, they must choose a minor portion and give up one or more of the benefits God has offered. For instance; I recently heard someone say, "I would rather have love than money." By saying this, they infer that wealth is somewhat evil. And I've also heard Christians say, "Well, having love is more important than having faith." And if you had to choose, love is more important, BUT, WHERE IS IT WRITTEN THAT WE CAN'T HAVE BOTH?

God wants us to enjoy ALL of His benefits. We deceive ourselves when we get caught up in this *either-or* thinking. You don't have to give up love to have wealth, or faith, or whatever! It is totally **YOUR** responsibility to be humble, whether you're rich or poor. The Bible clearly teaches us to "humble ourselves" in Matt. 18:4, Matt. 23:12, Luke 18:14, James 4:10, and 1ˢᵗ Peter 5:6. Even Jesus "humbled Himself." He was never forced to do it.

There are many men in the Bible that had it all. You can still be nice

Making Money With God

if you're rich! Poverty won't make you a nice person. There are plenty of poor people who are mean and nasty, as I'm sure you have found out.

One of the most powerful, loving ministers I've ever known is extremely wealthy. Even as a multi-millionaire, he passes out gospel tracts on street corners, and talks to people about being saved. The Holy Spirit helped him become wealthy by telling him what to invest in, and through doing business. We can have it ALL. God never said, "You must pick only one item."

Yes, it's true that you can't serve mammon (possessions, wealth, and riches) and God, but it is okay to have money that's serving you, as you serve God. Many in the Bible did this. Just be sure you're the master over the money, and not the other way around. This "out of order" scenario can happen with many other things as well. I'm thinking of a fellow I know who's owns a small business, but it really owns him. And I know other men who are owned by their ministries, or musical talents. What's controlling your life? Is it God, or something else?

You know, most ministers prefer to stay somewhere in the middle of any argument to avoid extremes, or offending anyone. They're often like the politician who wants to please everyone, so they pick the middle. So concerning prosperity, their view will usually be; "Christians should have a little more than enough to get by, but not too much more because they will surely self-destruct." After all, according to most preaching, we're only "unworthy, saved-by-grace sinners."

Forget the biblical fact that we're supposed to be new creations fashioned after Jesus. And forget that we're supposed to be partakers of His divine nature. Many preachers are going to keep you convinced you're only a "sinner saved by grace." This is tantamount to saying, "Even though you've been washed with soap, you're still dirty." You'll never develop a "Jesus mentality" without throwing such thinking away. Everyone will identify with the word "sinner," but few will actually assimilate the words "new creation" into their self-image.

As long as you believe you're only a "sinner saved by grace," you'll spend your days, and maybe even the rest of your life, trying to become a better person. But, if and when you realize you're a new creation in Christ, you might actually start DOING the ministry Jesus gave us to do. You might start walking as God intended instead of waiting for the day when you're finally "worthy."

Yes, the "middle" area is usually the favorite position because no one wants to be labeled an extremist. Somehow, we've all been convinced that having too much of anything is aligned with evil. For instance, if you believe "everyone is supposed to be healed," you're an extremist. Well, thank God Jesus didn't think like us, because He DID believe everyone was supposed to be healed, and proved it by healing them. But, does this apply to abundant provision? If you think so, again, you're an "extremist," and you're going to be criticized by everyone else.

Did Jesus take stripes on His back for everyone, or just a few? Did He die for everyone, or just a few? Did He become "poor" for everyone so they could be made rich, or just a few? Was the cross for everyone, or just a few? If you know the answers to these questions, then you'll know the answer to God's will concerning prosperity.

It's okay for God to be surrounded by extreme abundance because "He's righteous." So, what are we after we've been washed in the Blood? Jesus gave us God's righteousness in exchange for our sin, but that just isn't a reality to most; it's only good preaching. I'm not trying to get your heart set on "extreme wealth," but when a ship is way off course, you have make some extreme corrections in another direction.

I don't think it is necessarily wise for a minister to live an opulent lifestyle just because he can, but it's certainly not a sin either. It is always a good idea to consider the thinking of others if you're trying to reach them, even if they're thinking is wrong. In my opinion, this is part of the discipline and sacrifice ministers need to consider for the sake of reaching people, but again, this is only my opinion. Everyone has to give account for their own conscience. Paul tried to fit in with the people, as did Jesus, but we still need to know that our redemption is awesome in its provision, and that poverty thinking is NOT of God.

Our consciences have been trained to feel guilty if we have more than enough, or even just enough. The poor of this world have learned to resent those who have wealth because we don't teach them that they can have some, too. We lead them to believe that God prefers their poverty. Even some of our corrupt politicians push this guilt and resentment mentality as they continuously exploit the poor, making them believe they're actually poor because someone else is rich.

This gives the government a false justification for creating legislation against the rich, which in reality, is against everyone. This has happened in many Marxist/Communist/Socialist countries, but now America is being attacked by this same evil lie, only it's disguised as "social

Making Money With God

justice" and "fairness." Always be wary of such words, or phrases. True "justice" is usually the farthest thing from such deception. Any system of government that allows the achievement of great wealth is the best thing for everyone, because then anyone can do it, at least to the degree that their talents and efforts allow.

If you choke the wealthy, the not-so-wealthy will surely feel it, too, and even more so. They'll find this out when they go looking for jobs because poor people don't hire. To imply that "choking the wealthy (excessive taxing) will be better for the poor," is an absolute lie, and those who propose such things are usually aware or this fact, but they don't care. Such people are always interested in power and control, not the good of the poor. Do you think it's good to do everything for your children, when they should be learning to do for themselves?

Socialism is like starting with two people, one who plays the piano, and one who doesn't. Then, in an attempt to make them "equal," you bind up the hands of the one who has learned how to play, instead of simply teaching the one who doesn't. Wouldn't teaching them both how to play be a better solution? Then you would have two people who have useful abilities, instead of no one who can provide music, or whatever else is needed. It is truly an evil system. You can also tell this by the moral character of those who support it, or lack thereof.

The poor can obtain wealth, too, instead of resenting those who have it, if they would only learn how. There's plenty for everyone, but we're not supposed to believe this. We're supposed to believe that the rich got that way only by taking from the poor. The poor should quit listening to empty political promises, and those who lead them to blame the rich. They should go after their own wealth, with God's help. It will never come from government; and the less government takes of our money, the better it is for everyone, rich or poor.

It's true that the majority of Christians are unconsciously afraid of wealth. You can hear this when they speak. They may say "amen" when someone preaches on abundance, but most choose to believe that God is developing their character through poverty and lack, and He still has a long way to go. They usually leave church with some hope for the future, but rarely with the feeling that they qualify today. Many are afraid of too much grace for this same reason.

"Middle" thinking, and the associated poverty thinking, keeps us from expecting real abundance and success. It is often called the place of "balance," which usually means we're never going to *walk on the water*. Middle thinking says, "Sure, God heals, but not always;" and "Sure, God wants to meet our needs, but maybe not our desires; and certainly not in extreme amounts." "God is keeping us humble this way." This thinking would sound so right to most believers, but it is not even close to being right. Jesus proved this in His own ministry with extreme miracles and abundance that could not be contained. Remember the breaking nets of fish, and the leftover loaves?

ARE YOU BALANCED? I HOPE NOT!

What are you going to "balance" faith with; an equal measure of unbelief? The problem with the church idea of "balance" is this: Redemption from a position of eternal death IS VERY EXTREME! To be translated from total darkness to brilliant light is very extreme! But most of us like the dimly lit area in the middle. It's easier on our light deprived eyes. In spiritual reality though, this "gray, balanced" area doesn't really exist. This area of compromise is actually a part of the realm of darkness. Paul clearly shows this II Corinthians, chapter 6.

According to Paul, there is only righteousness or unrighteousness. These, of course, are two "extreme" opposites. There is no middle ground mentioned in this description of God's Kingdom, as compared to Satan's. There is only light or dark to choose from. Jesus said "you're either for me or against me."

This is why Jesus was so upset when Peter briefly suggested some compromise concerning God's will for Jesus to go to the cross. If we didn't already know how Jesus was going to respond to Peter's suggestion, many of us probably would have thought that Peter was "wise" to suggest such an alternative.

We should be equally upset whenever it is suggested that God's will is sickness, lack, or any other part of darkness. There was no lack or sickness in the Garden, because there was no sin. Well, has Jesus really redeemed us, or not? Has God washed our sins away, or not? Whenever someone suggests that you're sick because "God is teaching you something," "Get thee behind me Satan," would be a very appropriate response. It is not God making you sick, or "allowing" it! It is you who is allowing it, not God. Learn how to make it go away with faith and the authority Jesus has given us.

Making Money With God

Jesus was **righteously** extreme in everything He did, and the motivation was love. Our transformation from darkness to light is radical indeed. David was extreme in his zeal for God while all the "balanced" soldiers were afraid of Goliath. To go from wallowing with the pigs, to wearing a robe and ring of honor, as the prodigal son did, is quite extreme.

Had the average Christian been making the rules, the prodigal son would have had to stay in the bunk house for a number of years, and would probably never be fully reinstated to his former position. In the church, he would have to prove his "faithfulness as a steward" before he could have access to the father's wealth. We would always remember his sin and failure, but God chooses to forget and restore.

Have you ever studied the words *restore, redemption, salvation, righteousness,* and *forgiveness?* Your life will be changed if you do, if you actually believe what you find. The definitions of these words will reveal quite a different gospel from that which is normally put forth.

For example, the very word **"salvation" actually means to be healed, PROSPERED, made righteous, protected, delivered, lifted up, and saved.** One of the very first definitions of the word "righteousness" is *equity*, which has to do with prosperity. It has to do with assigning value to that which was formerly worthless. Paul said that we have actually been made God's very righteousness, because Jesus became our sin. Pretty cool, huh?

Many criticize "prosperity" without really knowing what has been taught about it, or even what the Bible says about it. Some will close their ears as soon as they hear the word "prosperity." They'll say the phrase "prosperity gospel" with disgust, implying that it is wrong or even some kind of abomination. This type of influence will often scare the sheep away from the truth. Throughout the Bible, prosperity has *always* been part of God's approval; and in the NT, we have His approval through Christ. There is nothing holy, moral, or virtuous within poverty.

Much of the reason that most Jews think that Christians are wrong is because Christians are foolish enough to believe that God wants them poor, or just barely making it. When Jews observe the typical, financially struggling, Christian, their opinions about Christianity are only strengthened. No Jew is ever going to think God endorses "hand to mouth" living. Virtually all of their historical heroes prospered tremendously when they served God, except during times of extreme persecution. Even then, they were usually cared for, and eventually restored, when they were living according to the Law.

The NT says that Christians should be making the Jews jealous by the way God is blessing them. Romans 11:11 Over the years I did a good bit of house painting to supplement my meager ministry income. And believe me; the Jewish home owners were not exactly jealous when I was painting "their" walls because I needed some of "their" money. They usually had plenty, too, amassed from not being religiously stupid, like I was. And likewise, the Jewish pawn broker I had to visit on occasion, due to meager preaching offerings, wasn't very impressed with my Christianity either. Who wants to serve a god that can't provide? Is that too real for you?

There's certainly nothing wrong with working hard for a living, but if it's not satisfying your idea of success, then something is wrong. It certainly was for me. A good friend of mine, Kevin Sullivan, says that one of the greatest revelations he's had in his life was the foolishness he felt when, as a minister, he delivered a pizza to a Hindu family that was living in an extremely nice home, while he was struggling to make ends meet. It was a major milestone in the changing of his thinking. Now, he's a published author and a much wiser man. Kevin didn't go home and wait for God to move, or *release* something. He simply started changing his own thinking, as you must.

Please pray and consider these thoughts before you reject anything you've read. You might be rejecting something that's true, simply because you have a stronghold in your own thinking. What if it is God's will to prosper us, but you stand against it because you think you're right, due to some "religious mindset" you've had for years?

Are you afraid of money because of the possibility of corruption? In reality, money only makes you more of what you already are, or reveals the corruption that already exists. Due to so many subtle implications, and without investigation, we automatically assume that God doesn't want us to have too much of anything, because of our human flaws. Again, many are afraid of grace for the same reason.

But, God doesn't think like us. He has declared: "Anything that can be shaken; **WILL BE!**" So forget this idea that God won't give us money because He knows we'll backslide if we get too much. This is just another tentacle of the spurious, "prove yourself" gospel. God wants

Making Money With God

you to be loyal to Him whether you have money or not, and if there is a problem with this, it already exists, even if you have no money at all.

Consider this: Since everything that "can be shaken, will be;" then it would make more sense for God to give us money than hide it from us. This way, any hidden corruption can be exposed which would be better for the individual in the long run. It was certainly better for the prodigal son.

Every secret thing will be revealed and you need to decide where you stand now, rich or poor. Money doesn't really mean very much to God anyway. We're the ones that make such a big deal out of it. Since the cross, the amount of money you have is more up to you, than God.

Determined people make things happen, while many of the chosen just keep waiting for that "stamp of approval," even though God has already given it. They don't believe this because their religious systems don't produce anything, and consequently, they think that God doesn't approve of them, just yet. Most preaching only reinforces this falsehood as everyone keeps searching for "the key."

The acquisition of money might expedite the exposure of a character flaw, or a sin condition, but it doesn't cause it. YOU must change your heart and your priorities! Of course, money and prosperity should never be our main interest, but that doesn't mean that it has not been offered in the atonement. Abraham was very rich, but to him it was just the way it should be. He used his money as a tool and a blessing to many others. He wasn't constantly consumed with getting more, but God caused it to come anyway.

You could see Abraham's lack of greed as he told Lot to select the land of his choosing, first. Then Abraham took what was left. David was the same way and he used much of his wealth to promote God's will. These men were not greedy, nor did they want what belonged to others, except for the time of David's weakness toward Bathsheba. This was not a money problem, though.

This weakness was probably due to the rejection he was experiencing from his own wife, Saul's daughter. The Bible reveals that she had some resentment toward David, possibly from Saul's influence, but this didn't justify David's sin.

WHAT IS REDEMPTION?

I'll say this again: Don't look at this wealth question from the perspective that most Christians use — that of performance — but look at it from the perspective of what Jesus has done for us through the act of redemption (to purchase back). In other words, **what did man start with; what did man lose when he fell; and what did Jesus regain?**

This is really the only way to look at the full picture of redemption. If you don't ask these questions, you'll only see a small portion of redemption. The church seems to only know about the forgiveness of sins, while overlooking all that was lost due to sin, and then regained at the cross. Some ministers teach that we don't have a full redemption (healing and wealth). But, they base this opinion on what they see, or don't see, in their congregations. This is an extremely faulty and backward way to develop doctrine.

Jesus proved the fullness of redemption time and again. He came to show us the Father's will and he never left anyone who desired healing, sick. If someone in your church has been prayed for, but not healed, it is **NEVER** because God didn't provide healing at the cross. You should be looking for the real reason they're not being healed, and it won't be God's lack of provision, His unwillingness to heal, or an incomplete atonement.

Usually, the answers are plain ole unbelief and ignorance. Faith can't grow very well in the soil of ignorance. People get upset if you tell them, as Jesus did, that they don't have enough faith. So the church has made up a truck load of reasons on why God didn't do what everyone was hoping for, but their excuses are never the real reason(s).

If easy, abundant, provision was lost due to sin, **and it was** (Adam had no lack whatsoever); THEN THIS AND ALL THINGS SHOULD HAVE BEEN RESTORED WHEN THE PRICE OF SIN WAS PAID AT CALVARY; AND THEY WERE! Our bodies will not live forever, but our formerly separated spirits, which have now been born again, will. Plus, we're now entitled to a better, glorified, body when we die, and there is no "sting" in death for the Christian.

All of the benefits of righteousness should be regained, because righteousness has been freely offered back to mankind! This is what the Prodigal Son's ring represented. But, the acquisition of these benefits requires faith. They do not just happen automatically.

Making Money With God

Unfortunately, many ministers, who preach that it is God's will that we prosper, make this blessing the result of THEIR set of legalistic guidelines, instead of faith and grace. And of course they claim that these are also God's guidelines. **But God stands ready to place a ring on your finger, and shoes on your, feet simply because you are His child!** No performance other than repentance and faith are necessary.

The father of the prodigal would have nothing to do with His son's offer to work, or *prove himself,* as a servant! And remember, Jesus and Paul both said that we would no longer be called servants.

Did God have to "trust you" before He would save you? Well, guess what; salvation included abundant provision before you ever did anything for God. The possibility for wealth has already been deposited in your account, if you're truly saved.

Do you really think that God trusts the rich people of the world more than everyone else? Is that how they got rich? Does God really trust the billionaire who funds every ungodly, liberal idea that comes down the pike? Was the Apostle Paul's occasional lack due to God's lack of trust in him, even though He used Paul to write most of the New Testament?

What about those who have become rich writing stories of sorcery, vampires, and delusion? Most of this garbage is written for children. Do you really believe their success comes from God, because He trusts them? Some of them have become extremely wealthy indoctrinating millions of children into the world of witchcraft, magic, and demons. They even help children believe that those who practice such things are the good guys. Are they really wealthy because God trusts them? This is what the church implies when we're told "God must trust us before He'll give us money." This thinking will always make you think you're not qualified.

"Oh, Brother Bruce, you're being way too strict on those authors; their books are just for fun." Yea, and so is the Book of Revelation when it says that Satan will deceive the whole world through *sorcery,* and harsh judgment will come. Have fun with that.

Such books only help to lower mankind into more darkness. They're bringing this world to the point where, through demon influence, they will totally reject God and all righteousness. Gee, do you think maybe that's happening now? Millions of children are being taught that wizards are better than Jesus, and witchcraft is better than real faith.

107

Jesus said it would be better to have a millstone tied around your neck and cast into the sea, than to lead children into such a life. I hope all such authors are enjoying their money while they can. Judgment is right around the corner.

Obviously, it does appear that money can be obtained without "God's trust," doesn't it? Let me ask you this: Did God know in advance that the "rich young ruler" would say no to Jesus? Well of course He did, but, isn't it interesting that he became wealthy even with God knowing that he couldn't be trusted? According to common church teaching, God never would have let him have wealth in the first place, but he had it anyway.

Would you trust someone who did what the prodigal son did? I don't know if I would, but apparently Jesus endorsed his immediate reinstatement, after he repented. God doesn't think like we do. Unlike you and me, He forgets our sins, and those of everyone else, too. Jesus' blood is constantly before Him on the "Mercy Seat," continuously reminding Him of the Cross. You should be very thankful that it is.

Maybe I've over-killed on this point, but this type of common teaching puts what we need (salvation) in the future; and it keeps everyone believing that they're not good enough for anything today. You can't be any more worthy of God's blessings than the Blood of Jesus has already made you.

IS GOD WEALTHY?

Why is it that we think it is normal for a child of Almighty God to be destitute and driving around in an old, worn-out minivan, while God is the wealthiest being in the universe? And we think this is for our own good. Christians are often employed by some rich sinner. It should be the other way around.

Why do we think it is okay for drug dealers, corrupt politicians, ungodly musicians, ungodly actors, and greedy debt dealers, to have plenty while those who serve God have little or nothing? Doesn't that seem out of order to you?

Many Christians have no clue that they are now "one spirit with the Lord," or that this joining puts the whole Kingdom of God at their disposal. Does "It is the Father's good pleasure to GIVE you the Kingdom," consist of a kingdom with minimal provision? Surely not!

Making Money With God

Do you know that the position of "heir" instantly gains access to everything God owns? The death of the "testator" has already taken place. The "Will" has already been executed and is intact forever! All challenges to the "Will" have been defeated and subdued! The "heirs" are fully entitled to everything listed in the Will, as desired by the benefactor (God).

A true heir has access to everything God has without having to do any of the steps required by most preaching. We form most of our ideas on God's provision based on what we see other Christians enjoying, or not enjoying, and they usually have no hard reality concerning the full scope of redemption. We often observe Christians who suffer, and even take pride in their pain and lack, and then we somehow determine that this must be God's will.

Our witness should be that of God's blessings on our lives, because Christ has made us righteous. Poverty is very common in areas of false religion, but it should never be a part of Christianity, unless it's the result of extreme persecution. Is poverty really something God intended true Christians to be known for? We should be known for our love and unselfish giving to every need that arises, and miracle provision for ourselves and others. We are called "priests," and the function of a priest is to be a connection to God for the people who don't know God.

Even in the worst of times we can be fed by the ravens. With God, in the middle of a desert, the rocks can turn into water. Food can be multiplied. Fish can jump in your boat. Quail can fly into your camp. Manna can fall from heaven. Armies can run away in fear, leaving their food and treasure. Gold can be taken from a fish's mouth. God can tell you what to do! Why are we ever worried about anything? JUST GET YOURSELF CLOSE TO GOD!

WEAKNESS OR STRENGTH

I just heard someone on the radio explain how their cancer has been such a blessing, because they are now able to minister to others who have cancer. This is such a common deception in the church world. This person even implied that God gave him the cancer for this purpose. Again, this is foolishness, but its common thinking in the church.

Why don't we try observing our prototype for ministry, Jesus? He never had cancer, but He still did a pretty good job of ministering to the diseased. He wasn't blind, yet He healed the blind. He never had leprosy, yet He cleansed the lepers. Apparently, He didn't find it necessary to be a victim before being able to be a good minister. Maybe, having the Holy Spirit's power is sufficient for this task.

If you were sinking in quicksand, would you want someone to jump in with you just so they could better understand your fear; OR WOULD YOU RATHER HAVE SOMEONE WHO CAN PULL YOU OUT? I'm betting it's the latter. Rescuing others is something that can only be done from a position of strength!

I wonder; does the above person, who now thinks he can minister to others better because he also had cancer, actually get the others healed of cancer? Or does he only offer "comforting words?" Please save your comforting words and excuses for the religious crowd, and give me some real power when I need help. I don't want to know why you think "God is doing this for my own good." I want what Jesus would really do in such a situation, as He did in the Bible.

You can't give much if you're poverty-stricken, or do much if you're sick. I've met thousands of Christians, many of whom were pastors, who dream about giving more but they just don't have anything to give. There are many good people out there, who want to do good, but they've just never been taught how. They never learned to make money, so their constant focus is on their own survival, and they believe this is God's will.

We should always believe the scriptures, and not the usual church thought. Psalm 112 says that "wealth" AND "riches" will be in the house of the righteous! What do poverty teachers do with that verse? I'm guessing they don't quote it much. It doesn't just say "wealth;" and it doesn't just say "riches!" But, it says "*both*" shall be in the house of the righteous! Remember; Jesus' blood has made you righteous, if you're a believer! So your house should be the "house of the righteous."

"For you know the grace of our Lord Jesus Christ, that, THOUGH HE WAS RICH, yet for your sakes he BECAME POOR, that YOU through His poverty MIGHT BE RICH!" (II Cor. 8:9) **JESUS DID THIS FOR YOU!** He became poor that you could become rich, just as He was made to be sin so that you could be made **the very righteousness of God!** (II Cor. 5:21). WEALTH IS PART OF THE ATONEMENT!

The Greek word used for "rich" in this verse means exactly that

Making Money With God

— "RICH," an abundance of everything. You may not believe this, but you can if you'll simply decide to accept what is plainly written. Don't let traditional, religious, thinking cancel the power of God in your life, as Jesus said it would.

A pastor's main job is not necessarily to show you how to prosper, but they should be able to at least let us know what's available in the atonement. Their main job is to keep you living a clean, holy life, while keeping your desire toward God. Their job is to lead people to Christ, and care for their flock. I know from experience that ministry usually doesn't leave much time to pursue business interests, but there still should be some measure of success to show as an example to the people.

Confusion concerning the things of God in any area will always stem from this one fact: Our understanding of the Kingdom of God is either based on God's written Word, as it is rightly divided, or it is based on man's limited understanding of the circumstances at hand, and man's attempt to then teach about what he does not understand.

The latter will produce, and has produced, all manner of false doctrine and speculations. Many of these have been accepted by the church as truth. We are usually so eager to open our mouths and be recognized, we often speak without knowing what we're talking about; and most of our listeners can't tell the difference.

We rarely make the Bible a part of us through diligence and understanding. This is why so many only teach what they have learned from other preachers. But, this ends up being like making a copy, of a copy, of a copy, on an old Xerox machine. Eventually it will be so blurred, no one can understand it. Sooner or later, through experience, we should be living what we preach, instead of always trying to set some future "standard."

Most preachers will agree that forgiveness is for everyone, but isn't it odd that many will say that healing is only for some, and wealth is for very few? BUT ALL THREE ITEMS CAME FROM THE SAME REDEMPTIVE SACRIFICE!

Just because someone prays, that does not necessarily mean that anything is going to happen. Prayer must contain real faith based on the knowledge of God's Word. We must know "how" to pray and what God's will is concerning the issue, which will be in agreement with His

Word. So many Christians simply do not know how to pray, or what God says about their request, or that they even qualify.

When there is no knowledge of God's will, the disappointed and afflicted parties begin to think that God doesn't want them to have the blessing(s) they need, or worse. And there will always be someone to help them believe that this affliction is for their own good. Job's "friends" are still very much alive, and they'll kill you if you listen to their reasoning. If your friends are telling you that your sickness and poverty are for your own good, go find new friends. Who needs the devil, if you have friends like that?

Do you even know what God's will is concerning your condition? Is God's Word going to be your final authority, or are you going to bow to some theologically diluted version of the gospel? Will it be God's written Word, or someone's religious opinion? Which will be your final authority? The one you choose will rule your life. Let me repeat that: The one you choose will rule your life.

The problem is on the receiving end, not on God's provision through the cross. Just because someone is in lack, or lives way below their possibilities, it does not mean that God did not provide much more at the cross. They simply haven't discovered God's will, or learned how to make money.

Every question you have is answered by that which was provided at the cross. And if it was provided at the cross, IT IS God's will for you to have it! The rest is simply a matter of learning how to "possess the land." The land of Israel was freely given to Abraham's children, before they had to fight to possess it, and keep it. And they're still fighting today.

It is our job to believe, and our job to keep Satan away from what God has given us. This is why Jesus gave us authority. It is not God's job to rebuke the devil, anymore. Read Luke 10:19; this is one of those "better promises." You should get my book on faith and authority.

Jesus did not exclude anyone from the provision of the cross. God does not select certain people to live in poverty. This is the result of the parenting they had, their training, and their life choices. Miracles and provision happen according to the faith on the receiving end. They are not the result of some ever changing, whimsical notion of a god who plays favorites with special, occasional blessings.

Jesus' finished work is "forever settled" in heaven, for "whosoever will." Did you observe that "the woman with the issue of blood," was

Making Money With God

not even noticed by Jesus until "AFTER" her **faith** pulled power out of his body? Other people in the pressing crowd were touching Jesus, but her "touch" connected with His power.

It is important to note that He didn't pick her, but she pursued Him. She wasn't just "hoping." **She had a plan and was determined to get what she needed.** And, she got it without even giving Jesus the chance to "approve" or "disapprove." You should meditate this fact, for a long while.

Jesus didn't just look around the crowd for someone He liked more than the others. He didn't turn and smile on her saying, "Today is your blessed day because I like you the more than these others." NO, He didn't even know who pulled the power out of Him, at first. She knew that Jesus had what she needed, and HER FAITH possessed it without any advance approval from God. She didn't have to prove anything first, as most ministers would have us do. In fact, most ministers would have kept her away from Jesus because she was breaking the rules. It was against the Jewish Law to be in a crowd with an issue of blood.

Faith would work even if God didn't love you, but He does, and He wants to give you the Kingdom. Quit trying to get God to like you, or approve of you, and possess what you need! The answer is "YES" to every promise, and God approves of everyone who is in Christ!

I spent my first twenty years of adulthood, in lack. I can tell you with certainty that my lack was due to ignorance, low self-esteem, poor money management habits, and listening to ministers who thought they had answers, but were no better off than me. As I was praying one day, God spoke to me said, "I've been trying to increase you for years, but you won't listen!" I looked back over my life and I could see that He had been trying to do exactly that, but I kept making the same dumb mistakes. A "poverty spirit" will keep you doing the same unfruitful things, again and again. I had to learn to listen, and make drastic changes.

God told me that big part of my problem was my circle of friends. They were all poverty minded as well, living hand to mouth and believing lies. If you play golf with people who are better than you, your game will improve. The same is true in the arena of wealth. Maybe you should start hanging with people who are successful.

God can provide for anyone if they will learn to hear Him, and if they'll quit trying to work religious formulas. In some countries,

113

it is easier to prosper than in others, but nonetheless, it can be done anywhere. Nothing is too hard for God. Some believe it would be impossible to teach people to prosper in certain Third World countries. They think the poverty is too extreme for even God. While nothing is impossible to the one who believes, it may be easier for those facing such an environment to simply relocate. It may take a miracle for this to happen, but God will help anyone who will seek Him.

In the Bible, God led several people away from hard conditions so that they could be blessed. He promises to feed those who trust in Him, even during a famine (Psalms 37:19). **God's leading is essential for obtaining His prosperity,** especially during hard conditions. If He tells you to stay where you are, He can show you how to rise above the poverty. Listen closely, though, because He may tell you to move. If the economy in your town has gone bust, plain old wisdom may dictate moving somewhere else. Some things are obvious without God's leading, but if you're not sure, pray.

Some preachers like to shout and claim, *"It doesn't matter what the economy is doing! And it doesn't matter what the stock market or the government is doing! Our blessings are based on God's economy!"* While such statements will usually get a rise out of the people, they're not exactly truthful. Don't be fooled by "grandstand" preaching. Yes, God is going to take care of us, but these other things CAN and DO affect us. Only preachers who can't afford to own stocks say such things.

While the streets are paved with gold in heaven, they may not be in such good condition in your town. They may even be riddled with potholes because the city doesn't have the money to fix them. God can give you wisdom to maneuver in and around a faulty economy, but again, it may be better to just move.

On the other hand, though, faulty economies can offer some extremely good financial opportunities, if you'll learn how to recognize them. Joseph got very rich off of a famine. "The wise man sees what is coming and prepares" (Prov. 22:3).

So, are all Christians supposed to have wealth? It's kind of a ridiculous question once you understand redemption. It's like asking, "Are all Christians supposed to be saved?" Or, "Was Jesus supposed to heal everyone that came to Him?" "Shouldn't He have said no to at least some of them?" The answer to wealth and these other things is not really up to God. It is up to each and every Christian. DO YOU WANT TO HAVE ABUNDANCE? Certainly, there are snares and traps associated with wealth, but nonetheless, God has provided the opportunities.

The poor usually have just as many hang-ups as the rich, and many other problems to boot. They often have their own form of "poor man's pride." So which pride is more wicked; the poor man's pride, or the rich man's? Again, Jesus stated that it is hard for those "who TRUST in riches" to be saved. Trust is the key.

God never intended for anyone, anywhere, to live in poverty and lack. After God put Adam in the center of a garden full of abundance, He didn't then create a barren dessert for the "unlucky" people. Some Christians probably think that God made the desert just for them. Did God make a mistake by putting absolutely everything Adam needed right at his fingertips? Well of course not! God intended for man to be well cared for. Why do you think the account of creation is even in the Bible? God wanted us to know what man had, before sin.

It is actually fairly easy to obtain a measure of wealth, **IF** you can just stay away from debt, which as you've probably found out, is not so easy. This is something our political leaders need to know, too. Learn to listen to those who have done it. Imagine being able to invest most of your paycheck every week, because you don't owe anyone. But most of us are working to pay back what we've already spent, and then some. If you were debt free, you would have so much in such a short period of time, you'd be giving it away everywhere.

If you don't want your share, that is your prerogative. It is not a sin to be poor, but it's not a sin to be rich either. It *IS* a sin to "love" money or "trust" in riches, though. IT IS TOTALLY YOUR DECISION! Wealth is available everywhere for the diligent and wise, and it will remain in the hands of those who are.

If you think you're in the condition you're in because God has been withholding from you, due to your performance, or His lack of trust in you; you might spend the rest of your life trying to win God's approval. Why not believe you're accepted NOW.

HOW MUCH IS TOO MUCH?

There are some who have accepted wealth as God's will, but not for ministers. They get really upset when they see a minister with a nice home(s) and/or car(s). I recently heard someone say they had a real problem with rich ministers, but of course they didn't consider that their own home, with an in-ground pool, would also seem extravagant to the financial class of Christians below them. And who's to say that the rich ministers didn't make their money through God's wisdom, an inheritance, or from a side business? Contrary to popular criticism, most ministers aren't stealing money from little old ladies, as many Christian critics would have you believe.

The problem with judging the wealth of others, a very hard-to-defend position, is this: **HOW MUCH IS TOO MUCH; AND WHO HAS THE AUTHORITY TO SAY?** Is it okay to have golden streets and pearly gates? Where are we supposed to draw the line, and who has the authority to draw it? Even Jesus promised a huge return, "**in THIS life**," on houses, lands, and/or anything else given up for the gospel; so what are we supposed to do with that verse?

But many Christians would have a real problem with the home, pool, and cars of the complaining Christian above, and they only have one house. Some would say, "Why couldn't they get a more modest home with an above-ground pool? Or why do they need a pool at all? How come their car has leather seats instead of cloth? And why do they need three cars?"

You see, it's all relative. The guy in the Chevy might complain about the guy with the Mercedes; and the guy on the bicycle might complain about the guy in the Chevy. Then the guy walking could complain about the guy with the bicycle. And EVERYONE complains about the minister who has his own plane. But wait a minute; maybe the plane is a good way to "redeem the time," as we're instructed to do. And maybe the plane is paid for by a corporate write-off. The critics never think of these things.

Everyone justifies their own position as they judge others, and what seems rich to you might be meager to someone else, or vice-versa. Maybe we should just take care of our own stuff, and our own heart.

I recently heard some silly country song about Jesus wearing a Rolex. And while the song was mostly criticizing the constant, ridiculous fund-raising on Christian TV, which I agree is a terrible representation of Jesus; the song still sent the message that Christians should be poor. It was also somewhat judgmental of anyone who wasn't poor. That message is just as wrong as what the "miracle sellers" are doing on TV.

Making Money With God

Personally, I think Christian TV "fundraising" does way more damage than good, because it's so constant. Nine out of ten times, that's what you're going to hear when you tune in, and it's usually done in very poor taste. Of course the TV guys are always claiming, "You can't buy a miracle," but then out of their next breath, they're testifying on how someone's gift to the TV station got them healed. They make the real gospel look cheap and phony to every one who is watching. But, they're always totally justified in their own eyes, and by their peers. Everyone else just rolls their eyes as they change the channel, including me.

I wonder; what kind of watch does this famous, and probably rich, country singer wear? Does he drive a car with air conditioning? Maybe some of us think he should drive without AC, and sell his records for less. After all, some people may not be able to afford his records. I would be willing to bet that he thinks the price of his records is no one else's business, and he would be right. Why should I care how much this singer has, unless I'm greedy, or full of envy? And why should he care if someone wears a Rolex.

Is a $300 dollar watch a sin, or is it only the Rolex that's evil? What about a $200 watch? Is this okay, or is $175 the limit? Or, do we have to wear a $10 Casio to be right with God? In fact, why does anyone need a watch at all since our cell phones have the time? Oh, but wait, maybe cell phones are too extravagant, too. Where does this end, and who decides what's okay?

You know, I remember when someone thought that my first cell phone really was extravagant, but that was before every teenager in the world got one. Maybe the minister, inspiring the above song, had been praying for a new watch. Maybe he had given away a really nice watch, or two. And just maybe, after a church service, a businessman came up to him and said, "God told me to give you this Rolex as a sign of His love and care for you." I've had such things happen to me before. If fact, on one occasion, God was displeased because I sold something He had given to me as an answer to prayer.

See if you can wrap your religious head around this: God actually forced me (literally) to drive a very expensive luxury car because he was trying to change my terrible, poverty minded, self image. I didn't want to drive it because I felt like I was showing off, but for several years, until God made it possible, I couldn't get rid of it, or get something else. The expensive car actually did open some doors of ministry for me, but it also closed some others. But, that may have been a blessing. Some will have a problem with this statement; but a new car, and new wardrobe, can do wonders for the way you feel about yourself.

Do you know what? Jesus might have worn a Rolex if it had been given to him from a loving heart. Do you remember the Bible story of the very expensive perfume? I once wore a homemade necktie because my youngest son made it for me in Sunday school. And even though it looks like it was made in Sunday school, it's still my favorite tie. The financial worth of the tie is irrelevant because I can still remember the look on his face when he gave it to me. Who are we to judge someone else's heart, or the property they possess?

Don't forget that it was Judas Iscariot who complained about the expensive perfume. He said, "This perfume should have been sold, and the money given to the poor." But, the Bible says that Judas didn't really care for the poor, he was just greedy. So, if you find that someone else's wealth is bothering you, maybe you are the one with the problem, not them. Someone needs to tell this to those who are in Washington, pretending to take money "for the poor."

Definitions of wealth are all relative. I remember when a friend told me that he and his wife were so low on money that they only had a thousand dollars in their checking account. He was extremely worried, but I was thinking, "Boy, I sure wish I had a thousand dollars in my checking account." We had two very different perspectives as he had been used to success, and I was just your typical Christian with a poverty spirit. Now a thousand dollars seems like nothing to me, but to many desperate Christians, it would be a small fortune.

Having an opinion about someone else's possessions really stems from a spirit of control and judgment because you "think" you know what is best for them, and you're ready to tell others how they should live. We should try getting our own lives in order. Let God judge those who you "think" are too rich. You should be happy for someone else's success.

Maybe the rich people think you're too poor, because you're lazy. Maybe they think you're not contributing adequately to the tax base, or various charities, so who is justified in either situation?

Control, or the perversion of control, has always been Satan's goal. This is what ungodly religion and politics are all about. And

Making Money With God

they're getting more ungodly every day. In both realms, there are those who desperately want to tell you how to live, spend, and die. People, especially the young, do need to be trained, but when it goes beyond this, a spirit of control can take over. God wants everyone to have a personal relationship with Him, without the influence of someone who is NOT authorized to persuade.

Control is all about swaying choices, and when it is ungodly control, as it usually is in government and false religion, your best interest is not a concern. "Control" is why ungodly politicians want to raise taxes, direct what's taught in schools, and remove as much parental management (the good kind), as possible. They think they are more qualified to make decisions about your money and your children, than you are.

There is a "good" kind of control, though. After all, someone has to drive the bus. But, this type of control is ordained of God, and it ALWAYS has in mind the best interest of those who are being led. This can be any leadership from church and government, to authority in the home, but even these arenas often end up out of order.

Unfortunately, we always justify ourselves thinking that *our* control is best of everyone, but this motive is often untrue, and self deceiving. I wish I had a dollar for every problem I've encountered in families because the woman was endeavoring to be the head of the house, instead of the man. Of course, the woman always thinks her control is for the best, because her "husband isn't leading the way she thinks he should." This is very common in Christian homes, and this type of control often cripples the growth of the children. We should all quit trying to be the Holy Spirit, and let people grow.

Getting back to controlling your own life; are you able to uproot the many non-producing trees in the garden of your mind to make room for the truth of redemption? This is your assignment and your faith for tomorrow, or the lack thereof, will depend on what you plant in your thinking today. Right thinking will bring you into God's promises. Can you adjust?

THIS BRIEF STORY SAYS IT ALL

There was a man who desperately wanted to migrate to America a number of years ago. He worked hard and saved as much as he could until he had enough to secure a ticket on a ship to America. He only had enough money for the ticket, but not enough for any food while on the ship. But he did manage to pack away enough cheese and crackers to last until the end of the voyage.

At dinnertime, he would sneak off to a closet or some private place and eat his cheese and crackers. Often, he would watch through the windows as the people in the dining rooms feasted on turkey, chicken, and steaks. He really wished he was in there with them, eating the wonderful-looking food, but he could not afford it. As they approached the American coast, he slipped off to his favorite closet for one last meal when the ship's steward opened the door and discovered him.

He explained, with some embarrassment, that he only had enough money for the ticket, but not the food. After shaking his head while laughing, the steward said, **"Don't you know that the food was included with the purchase of the ticket?"** Of course, the man felt like a fool when he realized he had missed out on all that good food. He could have been feasting with the others due to the "**package deal that was totally paid for,**" but he was unaware of the details of his ticket "*covenant.*" Do you get the point?

Are the angels shaking their heads at you, knowing what your covenant provides while you don't? It's right there in the Book!

DRINK YE ALL OF IT!

How many Christians go without because they don't know what's in their redemptive "covenant?" When Jesus served the wine at the Last Supper, He said, "This is the blood of **my covenant, DRINK YE ALL OF IT!**" He didn't say, "Just drink part of it, and I'll decide later if I should *release* some more." No, He fully intended for everyone to partake of the full redemption He was providing through His blood.

Every church thinks they're right. Every pastor thinks he or she is preaching "the whole counsel of God." Most ministers believe they are providing the truth, but just the very existence of so many denominations is proof that many of us are wrong, about many things. When you have so much disagreement, everyone cannot possibly be right. Do you know what Jesus provided at the cross?

I never think that God wants me excluded from health, wealth, or any other part of the salvation package. I've trained my mind and I won't allow it to ever consider such a thing. But most Christians are

Making Money With God

still waiting to be approved, and still wondering what God's will is concerning these things. They don't know what redemption is.

"JESUS BECAME POOR THAT WE MIGHT BE MADE RICH!" (II Cor. 8:9). Jesus was NOT setting an example of poverty for the rest of us! HE BECAME POOR TO BE AN **EXCHANGE FOR US!** He took your sin, your sickness, your mental anguish, AND YOUR POVERTY, so that you could have His righteousness, His health, His mind, and His riches.

God can give you wisdom that can bring wealth; and He promised to give wisdom freely. Wealth is probably not going to fall out of heaven, but the Holy Spirit can show you where it is, and how to get it. Do you have the courage to go after it? Or will you keep waiting?

The men in the Bible, who walked with God, became wealthy. Others recognized that God was with them because of their success. They could actually see it. There was no need to claim that the promises were "spiritually possessed" because everyone could see the actual result of the promise. There was no need for Abraham to pretend that his camel was going to last longer and need fewer repairs. He owned thousands of camels and everyone could see that he was blessed.

Today, even with a better covenant, you can usually spot the Christians because of their worn-out cars sporting "Jesus" bumper stickers and smoking tailpipes. They're advertising for the Kingdom of God as they travel the roads looking like they don't have a nickel. Just yesterday, I saw an old broken-down car on the side of the road with a bumper sticker that said, "Got Jesus?"

Maybe they were hoping that someone who really did have Jesus would stop and help. How many sinners do you think are drawn to Christ when they see how pitiful the Christians are? The poverty stricken sinners are probably thinking, "I must be saved, too!"

God is honored by success; and He honors with success. This is very clear throughout the Bible. It was always apparent when God was with someone and part of that picture was usually abundant provision.

Listen one more time to John's words in 3 John, 2. "Beloved, I pray ABOVE ALL THINGS that you may PROSPER and be in health, even as your soul prospers." John knew that both of these items, health and wealth, were included in "salvation." He was Jesus' closest disciple and friend, and he would not have been praying for something that was not God's will.

A. Bruce Wells

"And God is able to make all **GRACE** abound toward you; that you, ALWAYS having ALL SUFFICIENCY in ALL THINGS, may abound to EVERY good work" (II Cor. 9:8).

Having all sufficiency, at all times, in all things, can only be done with wealth. **The ability described in this verse is the very definition of being "rich."** Please notice that the ability comes from *GRACE*.

Wealth is in the package. Anyone who would say otherwise does not understand redemption. If the Father has wealth, so should the sons and daughters.

CHAPTER 7

VERSES

NOTE: SOME OF THE promises listed here were for keeping the Law, but, since we're "in Christ," who kept the Law and delivered us from the consequences of any failure to do so, we can still be recipients of these revised "better promises."

Psalm 32:8 I will instruct you and teach you in the way you should go: I will guide you with my eye.

Isaiah 42:9 Behold, the former things have come to pass, and the new things I will declare. Before they spring forth, I will tell you of them.

Isaiah 48:17 I am the Lord who teaches you to **profit**, and leads you by the way that you should go.

John 16:13 The Holy Spirit will guide you into all truth... and He will show you things to come.

Exodus 13:21 And the Lord went before them by day in a pillar of a cloud, to lead the way...

Psalm 23:2 ...He leads me beside the still waters.

Isaiah 42:16 I will lead them in paths they have not known, and I will make darkness become light before them, ... and I will not forsake them.

Isaiah 49:10 They shall not hunger nor thirst... for He that has mercy on them shall lead them... and shall guide them.

John 10:3 The sheep hear His voice, and He calls His own sheep by name... and leads them out.

Genesis 24:40 The Lord will send His angel before you and prosper your way...

Genesis 39:2 And the Lord was with Joseph, and he was a prosperous man...

II Kings 18:7 And the Lord was with him (Hezekiah), and he prospered wherever he went...

II Chron. 26:5 And as long as he (Uzziah) sought the Lord, God made him to prosper.

Psalm 35:27 Let the Lord be magnified, who has pleasure in the prosperity of His servant.

Psalm 37:23 The steps of a good man are ordered by the Lord.

Psalm 37:25 I have been young, and now I am old, yet, I have not seen the righteous forsaken, nor his seed begging bread.

Psalm 25:9 The meek will He guide in judgment...

Prov. 28:27 He that gives to the poor, shall not lack.

Psalm 48:14 For God will be our guide, even unto death.

Isaiah 58:11 And the Lord shall guide you continuously, and satisfy your soul in drought.

Phil. 4:19 But my God shall supply all your need according to His riches in Glory by (because of) Christ Jesus.

II Cor. 8:9 For you know the grace of our Lord Jesus Christ, that, though He was rich, yet for your sakes He became poor, that you through His poverty might be rich. (The context of this verse deals with money, which is more proof that provision is a part of redemption.)

II Cor. 9:8 And God is able to make all **grace** abound toward you, that you, always having *all* sufficiency in *all* things, may abound to *every* good work. (*"Always having all sufficiency in all things*," is actually the Greek definition for "being rich.")

Matt. 6:33 But seek first the Kingdom of God, and His righteousness, and all these things (clothing, food, wealth) shall be added unto you. (Don't read this verse through legalistic glasses as most of the church does. This verse isn't talking about earning God's blessings or working to prove your faithfulness before God will give you these things. Jesus was talking to people who had not yet experienced regeneration [being born again], and He was expressing that when you find God's kingdom, and God's righteousness, which instantly occurs when you're born again, you receive sonship and certain rights as an heir. This is what Jesus really meant as He talked with those who were trying to gain their own kingdom, and these other things, through their own efforts. This verse simply means, "Surrender to God, join His true family through Christ, and all these things are yours.")

Psalm 130:7 For with the Lord, there is mercy, and with Him is *abundant redemption*. (Easy provision was lost in the garden due to sin, so again, "redemption" would include *abundant provision,* as well as the forgiveness of sin.)

II Sam. 5:23 - 25 And when David inquired of the Lord (concerning the Philistines that wanted war), God gave David secret *instructions* saying, "Do not confront them directly, but circle around behind them near the mulberry trees, and when you hear the sound of movement in the tops of the mulberry trees, you shall rally your men for the Lord shall go out before you to smite them there. And David did as the Lord *instructed*, and smote the Philistines there...

II Kings 6:10 And God sent and warned the king of Israel (of the Syrian king's trap), not once, nor twice...

A. Bruce Wells

Matt. 2:12 And being warned by God in a dream, that they should not return to Herod, they departed to their own country.

Matt. 2:13 Behold, the angel of the Lord appeared to Joseph in a dream saying, "Arise and take the child and his mother and flee to Egypt…"

Acts 10:22 And Cornelius was warned (instructed) by God, through a holy angel, to send for Peter…

Hebrews 11:7 By faith, Noah, being warned by God of things not yet seen, moved with fear…, and saved his house…

Matt. 17:27 And Jesus said to Peter, Nevertheless… cast a hook into the sea… take the first one that comes up… and you shall find a piece of money in his mouth…

Acts 16:6 They (Paul & Silas) were forbidden by the Holy Ghost to preach in Asia.

Acts 16:7 They assayed to go into Bithynia, but the Holy Spirit would not allow them.

Acts 16:9 And in a vision at night, Paul saw a man of Macedonia saying, "Come to Macedonia and help us…"

Acts 10:19 And while Peter thought on the vision, the Holy Spirit said to him, "Three men are seeking you; arise and go with them for I have sent them…"

Acts 8:26 & 27 And the angel of the Lord spoke to Philip saying, "Arise and go south on the road down to Jerusalem, in the desert…" and he went and saw a man of Ethiopia…

Acts 8:29 And the Holy Spirit said to Philip, "Go and join yourself to that chariot."

Act 9:9, 10 & 12 And the Lord said to Ananias, "Go to Straight Street, to the house of Judas, and ask for Saul of Tarsus… for he has seen you coming to him in a vision…"

Making Money With God

Acts 18:9 & 10 Then spoke the Lord unto Paul in a vision by night, "Be not afraid to speak here, for I am with you and no one will hurt you... for I have many people in this city."

Acts 22:17 & 18 While in a trance, I (Paul) saw Him (the Lord) saying to me, "Hurry and get out of Jerusalem, for they will not receive your testimony concerning me, there!"

Acts 22:21 And God said to me (Paul), "Depart, and I will send you to the gentiles."

Acts 23:11 And the Lord stood beside him and said, "Be of good cheer Paul..."

GOD CAN, AND DEFINITELY WILL,
SPEAK TO HIS PEOPLE!
HAVE FAITH!

Do you know that purchasing real estate or making other investments at an early age, is a key indicator that economist use for predicting future wealth?
YOU'RE NOT GETTING ANY YOUNGER!

ALWAYS REMEMBER:
NOTHING WILL CHANGE UNLESS YOU CHANGE IT,
AND YOU WON'T CHANGE UNTIL YOU RENEW YOUR MIND.

A. Bruce Wells

Write us and let us know if this book has helped you.
Email: FeetBeautiful@comcast.net

See other books by this author at: www.brucesbooks.com
Or go to: www.Authorhouse.com

Bruce is gifted speaker, teacher, and minister, available for speaking to
your church, group, or
radio/TV show. Contact him by email at:
FeetBeautiful@comcast.net

BEAUTIFUL FEET MINISTRIES, INC.
P. O. Box 6061
Stuart, FL 34997
www.BeautifulFeetMinistries.com

ABOUT THE AUTHOR

A. Bruce Wells was born in Louisville, KY in 1954 and became a Christian in 1977. He began working in the ministry in 1979 and in 1983 left secular employment for full time ministry. That same year Bruce formed BEAUTIFUL FEET MINISTRIES, INC., the non-profit organization under which Bruce would work as a traveling minister, missionary, and pastor.

Invitations to speak to a large variety of churches has taken Bruce to 48 states and a number of foreign countries including New Zealand, Australia, Peru, and England. His teachings on Easy Evangelism have been requested and used in quite a number of countries due to the popularity of the series. Many pastors have said that it is the best teaching series on evangelism they've ever heard and it has helped thousands of inexperienced Christians lead others to Christ.

Bruce and his wife Marsha love being around the water and they enjoy the perfect winter weather of southern Florida. They have lived on the east coast of FL since 1999 with their 3 sons, Joel, Nathan, and David, all musicians like their dad, and Bruce still travels worldwide in ministry. He continues to write and enjoys playing, writing, and producing worship music. Life is good.